HIS LORDSHIP

My Internship Experience with Chief Justice P.S Dinesh Kumar at the Karnataka High Court

Foreword by
Hon'ble Chief Justice of India (Retd) Shri MN Venkatachaliah

KRITHIK KAILASH

INDIA • SINGAPORE • MALAYSIA

Contents

Date: 23.02.2024

<u>CERTIFICATE</u>

This is to certify that Mr. Krithik Kailash, pursuing 10th Semester of 5 years B.A.LL.B in Christ (Deemed to be University), Bengaluru, has completed his internship under my guidance from 26.09.2022 to 23.02.2024 at the Principal Bench, High Court of Karnataka, Bengaluru.

During this period, he has attended Court proceedings in the High Court. He has also attended official events and diligently performed the duties assigned to him. Krithik has assisted me in preparing notes for a diverse range of matters, including Writ Petitions, Writ Appeals, Regular First Appeals, Income Tax Appeals, Customs Appeals, Sales Tax Revision Petitions, and Company Appeals.

His performance is excellent.

I wish him a bright future.

(P.S.DINESH KUMAR)
CHIEF JUSTICE

Shri.MN Venkatachaliah
25th Chief Justice of India
Sir M.N Krishna Rao Road
Bengaluru - 560006

June 7th – 2024

Foreword

'HIS LORDSHIP' is an affectionate tribute by a grateful pupil to his master so sensitively conveyed about a near-ideal master-pupil relationship. It is also a subtle message to the seniors of the profession about heightened expectations for the modern juniors in the legal profession. Chief Justice Shri P.S Dinesh Kumar comes through the pages as an ideal, compassionate, liberal and erudite mentor setting a new standard for the seniors in the profession towards the new aspirants. The Book has a charming get-up with telling photographs that enrich the narrative. It is thoughtfully dedicated to the gracious lady behind the Chief Justice.

Author Krithik Kailash's case-notes indicate a sharp legal mind and promise of an erudite career. I wish him every success.

M.N.Venkatachaliah

Former Chief Justice of India

Justice Shivaraj V. Patil

Formerly Judge,
High Court of Karnataka,
High Court of Madras,
Chief Justice, High Court of Rajasthan,
Supreme Court of India and
Member, National Human Rights Commission

" Sparsh',
254,18th Cross,
Sadashivanagar,
Bangalore-560 080

Review

Mr. Krithik Kailash requested me to say a few words by way of review of his book "HIS LORDSHIP – My Internship Experience with Chief justice P.S. Dinesh Kumar at the Karnataka High Court". Having read this book, I am happy to record my appreciation of the work done by Mr. Krithik Kailash. This compilation shows that he was keen to learn and gain experience while doing his internship with Chief justice P.S. Dinesh Kumar at the Karnataka High Court. He has captured important events in which Chief Justice P.S. Dinesh Kumar participated. He has also stated about certain legal aspects and the experience gained by him. He gratefully acknowledges the lessons he learnt and the experiences he gained during his period of internship. This book shows that the Chief Justice guided him and he sincerely assisted him to the best of his ability. There was amiable and cordial relationship between him and the Chief Justice and also with the family members. The various events captured in this book with photographs make the book interesting and impressive. My impression about him is that he is humble and hardworking which will enable him to rise further in the profession. I always hold the view that hard work, honesty and humility get blessed by divinity.

I wish Mr. Krithik Kailash all well in the days ahead.

(JUSTICE SHIVARAJ V. PATIL)

Acknowledgements

Acknowledgement ensures the presence of personalities who made this book a reality for the scholarly world. I deem it a privilege and great fortune to have received the blessings of Former Chief Justice of India Shri M.N. Venkatachaliah in the form of a foreword.

I express my gratitude to Chief Justice Shri P.S Dinesh Kumar for imparting valuable legal lessons. Every day of observation provided me with an insightful learning experience in understanding the role of Judges within our democratic polity. I am deeply indebted to Smt. Jayashree Pratinidhi for enabling me to craft each page of the book with divine guidance during this constitutional journey.

In the first week of September, my parents, Dr. Kathirvel and Mrs. Arthy Lakshmi encouraged me to apply for judicial internship at the Karnataka High Court. The sacrifice and determination of my parents to provide quality education to their children have pillared our progress for over two decades on Planet Earth. I'm thankful to my teachers and friends for being a constant source of strength and support throughout the process of completing this book. Lastly, I'd like to express my appreciation to Notion Press for their creative ideas in publishing this book.

Dedication

Book Dedication to Smt.Jayashree Pratinidhi

I dedicate this book to Respected Jayashree Madam, whose invaluable guidance and benevolence are immeasurable for me to express in written words. 'Madam Justice' is an apt description for the role played in the life of Hon'ble Chief Justice P.S Dinesh Kumar, who attributed his success and strength to family members in the farewell speech at the Karnataka High Court.

Respected Jayashree Madam's fascination for art and craft can be seen from the innumerable art work borne out of innate creativity and imagination possessed by artists par excellence. The flair for writing poems in three languages, namely Kannada, English and Hindi, covers an ocean of topics ranging from nature's gifts bestowed upon Planet Earth to the humdrum of daily life.

A divine and pious personality who embodies purity in life. I embarked on writing this book to treasure my experience with 'His Lordship' who lives a noble life by dedicating it to 'Madam Justice'.

Family Members

Left to Right – Mr. Amogh, Mrs. Madhuri, Mr. Madhav, Smt.Jayashree madam in the Office of Chief Justice P.S Dinesh Kumar.

Mr. Madhav –

A Chartered Accountant by profession has an excellent track record in the academic field. I recollect an anecdote by His Lordship that Mr Madhav stood first in the class time and again to the envy of others who could not better the performance despite tremendous competition. A dedicated and focused personality beacons the rich traditions followed by His Lordship.

Mrs. Madhuri –

The daughter of His Lordship is an 'Advocate' by profession with a keen interest in law and literature. A kind, compassionate and graceful personality symbolizing the qualities of the name 'Madhuri'. I am grateful for the support and guidance extended during my internship period.

Mr. Amogh –

The 'Solar Man', as described by His Lordship, works in a reputed solar company in Bangalore. The Son-In-Law of His Lordship is a cricket enthusiast devoted to family and work. I am grateful for the valuable guidance extended during my internship period.

About the Author

Profile Photo

Mr. Krithik Kailash recently completed his law degree at Christ University, Bengaluru and received the 'Best Orator of the Year' award during his schooling at Sarala Birla Academy. In September 2022, he felt a strong desire for a judicial internship, leading him to intern at the Office of Chief Justice P.S Dinesh Kumar. He worked extensively on case analysis and research combined with field visits to the Courts in Karnataka.

Kailash's reading habits are extensive, with the Bhagavad Gita deeply influencing his perspective on leading a purposeful life He attributes his strong values of spirituality and inner strength to his parents, for which he is grateful. Additionally, Kailash is enthusiastic about playing both tennis and football.

The first book named 'People's Governor' published in the month of October, 2023 by Mr. Krithik Kailash documents his lifetime experiences as an intern at the Office of Lieutenant Governor Dr Kiran Bedi who described Kailash as a 'young man of character and strong value systems' in a tweet shared across various social media platforms. Chief Justice P.S Dinesh Kumar describes him as a 'young, energetic, and smart budding lawyer'. Former Chief Justice of India Shri.M.N. Venkatachaliah 's foreword in the present book vividly encapsulates the internship experience at the Karnataka High Court.

A Destined Journey

Receiving the Internship Certificate from His Lordship at the Karnataka Judicial Academy.

A new era of educational experience began post-covid pandemic as Universities across India opened up for offline classes. In the fourth year of law school, the senior batches were allowed to do part-time internships to upscale the understanding of law in the practical world. I began to explore the possibility of a judicial internship at the Karnataka High Court.

I believe that judicial internships provide a platform to understand the role played by the bench in administering justice to the litigants. I learnt that the Establishment Branch is the guiding point for students seeking internships. I immediately took a transport to the High Court with a firm belief that I would get an opportunity to work in the chambers of a Judge at the Karnataka High Court.

The police officer at Gate No – 2, reserved for judicial officers and advocates, asked me to take a longer route to enter the premises. As the guards asked questions about my internship, I remained persistent to go to the Establishment Branch. I knew none and sought the guidance of advocates and staff to meet Mr. Harish to seek a judicial internship. He politely asked me to request another individual in the room. I was taken aback by the kind conversation by the woman staff, who intended to know my preference for the chamber of a Judge. I left it to the officer to select the chamber.

The officer immediately took the phone and contacted the Private Secretary of Hon'ble Justice P.S Dinesh Kumar. After the call, I received instructions to contact the chambers for further confirmation of the internship opportunity. The guided path to the office led to my meeting with Private Secretary Mrs Sudha, who asked me to meet His Lordship Hon'ble Justice P.S Dinesh Kumar. I walked into the room with my Curriculum Vitae and other documents for identification.

His Lordship asked about my educational background and ability to do research-oriented work on nuances of the law. After the brief interview, I received the confirmation letter to begin my internship at the Karnataka High Court in the blessed chambers of Hon›ble Justice P.S Dinesh Kumar. Devout prayers by my mother Mrs. Arthy Lakshmi and Father Dr. Kathirvel, at Namakkal's Lord Anjaneya temple, led me to the Chamber of Hon'ble Judge.

I learnt that His Lordship is an ardent devotee of the temple and often travels to Namakkal to receive the blessings of the presiding deity. As I reflect on the day of receiving the internship confirmation, one striking moment is the decision of the officer at the Establishment Branch to choose and dial the Office of His Lordship among the number of judicial chambers at the High Court. An ordinary day became extraordinary with destiny's play to become a judicial intern. My parents received the news of the internship confirmation with great surprise and joy. A new chapter awaited in my educational career.

I observed the functioning of Indian Judiciary as a separate branch of Government with Judges possessing absolute independence and authority in the decision-making process to meticulously deliver a Judgment in accordance with the law. The opportunity to witness the dictation of judgment by His Lordship was a particularly enlightening experience, opening new avenues of thought for understanding the art of judgment writing. The transition from the position of a Judge to Chief Justice of Karnataka gave me a practical understanding of the appointment process envisaged as per the Memorandum of Procedure and judicial precedents.

My travel with the Chief Justice for official events across Karnataka gave me a glimpse of India's unified judicial system, which is a binding force for a geographically vast and diverse nation. I connected with Karnataka's rich heritage and culture during my official visits with the Chief Justice. Pomp and ceremony in welcoming newly appointed Judges whereas solemn farewell to the Judges demitting office marked a branch of Government which has steadfastly protected the rights of people since the enactment of the Indian Constitution. My internship experience with the Chief Justice of Karnataka encapsulates a lifetime experience gained as a law student with a plethora of lessons to be practically applied for achieving the true purpose of my internship journey.

Chapter 1

Legal Voyage

Hon'ble Chief Justice P.S Dinesh Kumar

The first chapter covers my extensive conversations with Hon'ble Chief Justice P.S Dinesh Kumar on the turning points in life and insights into the fascinating legal journey documented over the course of my internship. I have strived to present the extraordinary career of His Lordship in a simple and forthright manner to benefit the readers.

Hon'ble Chief Justice of Karnataka, Shri P. S Dinesh Kumar, was born on February 25th, 1962, as the son of Shri.P.S. Srinivasacharya, who also served as a District and Sessions Judge. His Lordship's role model was his father, who embodied an intellectual aura and divine faith. The treasured conversations ranged from law to philosophy, covering a wide range of subjects with astounding expertise in each field.

His Lordship with Father Shri. Shrinivasacharya Pratinidhi [File Photo]

His Lordship's father devoutly followed the 'Bhagavad Gita' by chanting each of the eighteen chapters daily and adhering to Lord Krishna's teachings. The turning points in His Lordship's life began at a young age while being under the guidance of his maternal uncle for going to the hometown school which taught valuable lessons such as learning to live away from his parents and to share with others in life. The decision to join National High School became pivotal in life's journey. Notably, His Lordship earned the National Merit Scholar Certificate, where the first 100 ranking students in SSLC (Class X) were awarded merit scholarships. However, children of those drawing higher salaries were given the Certificate. His Lordship made the hard decision not to join medicine after receiving both engineering and medical seats and immediately joined law college upon receipt of a provisional degree in engineering.

His Lordship stands before the Rolls where father Shri.Shrivasacharya Pratindhi presided as a District and Sessions Judge – Mandya

The legal voyage began with the decision to practice in the Karnataka High Court and join the Office of Shri Shivaraj V Patil, Former Judge of the Supreme Court of India. Justice Patil and His Lordship's father shared a unique bond. Justice Patil's first appearance as a lawyer was in the father's court. Hon'ble Chief Justice P.S Dinesh Kumar recollected the kindness and affection shown by Justice Patil for accepting him as a Junior, though the Office was packed with 24 Juniors, with His Lordship being the 25th at the Office. A dinner meeting used to be arranged every year where Justice Patil and his family were invited. In one such function, His Lordship presented a nice rosewood table with 25 elephants carved on it!

His Lordship with Former Attorney General of India Shri.Soli Sorabjee

The call to join the legal panel of Central Government became a momentous decision in the legal journey. His Lordship had a great experience working with Mr. Soli Sorabjee, who would reach Bangalore in the evening and hold a conference immediately upon arrival. He was one of the most brilliant lawyers with excellent court craft and would appreciate if grounds were put in bullet points. Shri. Soli Sorabjee had a special affection and would involve His Lordship in almost every case he appeared, no matter who had briefed him. His Lordship had the privilege of keeping the jacket and gown, making them available for every hearing. After the hearing, Shri. Soli Sorabjee would promptly hand them over to His Lordship.

His Lordship shared that it was a great feeling to receive a copy of the treasured letter that Mr Sorabjee wrote to the then Union Law Minister Shri Jana Krishna Murthy to be appointed as part of the Additional Central Government Standing Counsel in the year 1998.

His Lordship was appointed as Senior Standing Counsel in the year 2003, with a thrilling experience of being the Head of the panel for Central Government Lawyers and the opportunity to appear in several important matters. As the Senior Panel Counsel for the Central Bureau of Investigation (C.B.I), His Lordship had a chance to appear in various high-profile corruption cases, such as those against a Former Chief Minister and a Former Union Railway Minister.

As the Senior Standing Counsel for BSNL, His Lordship recollected that BSNL was slapped with a tax of about 3000 Crores by the State Government and was challenged successfully in the High Court with the demand being quashed in the high-profile matter. The Union Public Service Commission engaged His Lordship in a large number of cases, with the most exciting being a batch of cases by KAS officers, which is now an authority often quoted as the MV Thimmaiah case. His Lordship represented the University Grants Commission (UGC), All India Council for Technical Education (AICTE), National Council for Teacher Education (NCTE), Standing Counsel for Karnataka State Power Transmission Corporation (KPTCL), Karnataka State Road Transport Corporation (KSRTC), Bangalore Electricity Supply Company (BESCOM), Bangalore Development Authority (BDA) in the illustrious legal voyage. As a Mediator and a trainer in Mediation, His Lordship was enrolled as a trainee in the first batch of mediators trained by American mediators. On the first day after training, there were three cases referred to His Lordship and all got settled resulting in a surprising news at the event.

His Lordship appeared in important incidents in different High Courts and the Supreme Court in matters concerning the appointment of Director, C.B.I, Disinvestment of ITDC Hotels, Defamation case against the Union Finance Minister etc. On an application filed by Mr

Dinakar [IPS, IG & DGP], Karnataka, the Central Administrative Tribunal - Bangalore had set aside the appointment of Mr Raghavan, IPS, as the Director of CBI. On behalf of the Union of India, His Lordship was asked to file a Writ Petition. Attorney General for India, Mr Soli Sorabjee, appeared in the case and was assisted by Mr Kirit Raval, Additional Solicitor General, Mr. VT Gopalan, Additional Solicitor General, South, Chennai and His Lordship. The CAT's order was stayed by the bench headed by the then Chief Justice, Hon'ble PV Reddy. In the matter concerning ITDC Hotel, the Central Government had disinvested its stake in ITDC Hotels where Mr. Lalit Suri had purchased Hotel Ashok, Bangalore. The Union of India, represented by Shri. Soli Sorabjee succeeded in the case challenged by Workmen.

His Lordship represented the then Union Finance Minister Yashwant Sinha in a defamation case. The Jindal Workmen filed a private complaint against the Minister, alleging that he had called the owner of Jindal Aluminium a 'mad person'. The Complaint was dismissed in the Magistrate's Court, and the City Civil and Sessions Court, Bengaluru, dismissed the Revision Petition. The Language Policy of the State was a long-drawn case where the State Government introduced a policy to make the Kannada Language compulsory for students from Class 1 to 4. Former Chief Justice of Kerala, Shri UL Bhat, led the case with His Lordship representing Karnataka Unaided Schools Management Association.

In his experiences with distinguished law officers in the country, His Lordship recalls the memorable association with Mr Mohan Parasaran, Former Solicitor General for India as a fine lawyer and a great human being to work on various cases, including the most critical BSNL matter. His Lordship had the opportunity to deal with almost all types of cases while heading both single and division benches as a Judge and Chief Justice of the Karnataka High Court. Several of them were important matters which involved interpretation of law.

The Hon'ble Chief Justice Shri P.S. Dinesh Kumar with Governor of Karnataka after the swearing-in-ceremony on February 3rd – 2024.

His Lordship narrated the moving gesture of gratitude with folded hands in open court in a bank case where several depositors got a portion of their hard-earned money. The matter was pending for a long time, and His Lordship was determined to resolve it, and by divine grace, the matter was resolved. In a matrimonial case, the husband was harassed with criminal cases and lost his overseas job. As he had no money to engage a lawyer, he argued party in person and succeeded. On the date of pronouncement, His Lordship observed tears rolling down his cheeks. His Lordship sums up several such momentous events as a satisfying experience of working true to the Oath of Office in delivering justice to numerous citizens. As the Chairman of Karnataka State Legal Services Authority, an all-time high number of about 25 lakh cases were solved during a mega Lok Adalat.

During the brief stint as the Chief Justice, His Lordship toured several districts and presided in both Dharwad and Kalaburagi benches, whereas, on the administrative side, 70 officers were promoted as District Judges with one order. As the Presiding Officer of the Securities Appellate Tribunal, His Lordship mentions that it has a bar of erudite lawyers who come prepared and that working on the new assignment has been a great pleasure.

His Lordship encapsulated the legal voyage as – 'Grace of Almighty, Commitment and Hard work.'

Chapter 2

Lessons in Observation

Official Chamber of His Lordship

This chapter covers the ocean of experiences learnt by the power of observation. Observation is a tool to enhance the power of knowledge. Each day, I observed the court proceedings from the space reserved for court officers. Judges and Advocates play an important role in the established process for administering justice within our democratic framework. The inquisitive questions put forth by Hon'ble Justice P.S Dinesh Kumar needed a strong understanding and grasp of law by the advocates. The experienced advocates with crafty answers impressed the Bench on complex questions of law, indicating that preparation is the key to successfully arguing a case. The fierce arguments by each counsel in citing precedents and established rules along with facts and circumstances provided an intellectual atmosphere. His Lordship diligently noted the counsels' arguments for writing an elaborate judgment. The conversations between the Judges in the division bench were closely observed by the advocates for hints in channelling their arguments to gain a favourable outcome. The court hall observations included the role played by the Court Officers in calling out the listed cases as per the Cause List.

A Court Officer assisted His Lordship by placing the necessary bare acts and paper books concerned with the case. One officer was deputed to update the outcomes in the computer system, whereas another officer readily noted His Lordship's orders in 'shorthand' to note the instructions quickly. The perfect coordination between the court officers in assisting the Bench indicated the extensive training received in performing their responsibilities to the best of their ability. His Lordship lauded the advocates who were well prepared by presenting the cases in a fair and prudent manner. I recall that advocates who sought to convince the Bench without due preparation were taken aback by the gush of questions put forth by His Lordship. An advocate who appeared online without knowing the facts and circumstances in a case received a fine of Rs.2000 directed to be paid towards the State Legal Services for ensuring that precious judicial time is saved during future appearances.

Penning Down My Observations

The repeated requests for adjournments displeased the Bench as litigants were to bear the brunt of the delay in getting justice. Advocates seated in the courtroom were quickly flipping through numbered pages to present their case before the Bench. Packed courtrooms led to advocates standing on both sides of the aisle with many placing and moving files from the allotted spaces. The ever-moving matters kept the court hours packed with intellectual prowess that was both refreshing and tiring in long tax matters. His Lordship's simplistic understanding of the visibly complex concepts reflected the rich experience gained from decades of practice as a distinguished advocate at the High Court of Karnataka. The easily readable judgement written using simple jargon by His Lordship remains a remarkable learning experience. As an intern, I understood the fascinating process behind the writing of judgements in the scholarly world of Indian Judiciary with His Lordship immersed in the dictation of the matter before consideration.

The rich knowledge possessed by His Lordship ensured the drafting of a quality judgment. The judgement writing involved a solemn process to uphold the constitutional responsibilities vested by the Indian Constitution where Judges hold the divine responsibility to protect the heart and soul of Indian democracy. Indian Judiciary steadfastly continues to guard the rights of citizens. His Lordship's view on the life of a judge can be described as a 'hermit in the forest'. I would like to recall vivid memories from the early days of my internship at the Karnataka High Court. An interview was scheduled to be held with His Lordship for meeting the volunteers for Legal Aid Services. Advocates enrolled themselves to serve the litigants who may not possess the ability to pay for filing their case. His Lordship asked me to be seated in a chair and observe the interview process. I recalled the energetic participation of numerous dedicated members, including a specially-abled person who brought a bouquet and shawl for His Lordship. As the person lifted the bouquet and shawl, His Lordship immediately got up from the chair and walked to the middle of the room to accept the greetings with kind words and appreciation, leaving a profound impact on the individual. It left an indelible mark on the life of an advocate who will cherish a friendly and warm conversation with His Lordship. The ability to ensure that each member leaves with memorable moments highlighted the importance of developing essential qualities in our daily lives.

My observations revolved around a number of official meetings conducted by His Lordship, heading various administrative committees scheduled after court hours. The duration of the meeting depended on the number of listed subject matters for the day. I understood the essence of a judge's life rooted in service of the people. It is a perpetually moving life at the Karnataka High Court. Senior advocates, along with juniors, shift from court to court with cases moving at a fast pace, ensuring a continuity in the vision laid down by our founding fathers of the Indian Constitution while separating the Judiciary as an organ of government. The application of legal jurisprudence and the construction of judgements remain steadfast in my observatory lessons.

Chapter 3

Research Work

Penning Down Notes for Research in the month of January – 2024

My first day of work at the Karnataka High Court began with research on the nature of an amendment to the Customs Law. His Lordship instructed me to identify whether the amendment was retrospective or prospective in nature. As the session began in the afternoon, I extensively researched the Customs Department's official website to determine the nature of the amendment. As an Intern, His Lordship asked me to read the factual matrix of the case and share my opinion on the substantial questions of law before the Court. This exercise gave me a better insight into the judicial interpretation process based on legal precedents.

I had the opportunity to research on judicial decisions about 'Show Cause Notices' during my internship. I had been delegated the duty to research His Lordship's scheduled addresses in various forums. Throughout my internship, it enabled me to expand my horizon of knowledge and understanding of multi-faceted topics. I had the opportunity to learn from the crucial lessons imparted by legal stalwarts.

Presenting the Research Work to His Lordship

It is fascinating to note that an excerpt from the book "Soli Sorabjee, Life and Times tells us that" in the first ten important cases that he appeared, Sorabjee was led by a senior and did not offer any independent arguments in Court. Naturally, the senior advocate he was 'led by' most often in his cases in the early days was his own senior, Kharshedji for four years into his practice. As a junior, the majority of the briefs that Sorabjee received were those in which he had to stand up in a packed courtroom, face the judge, make his arguments, and try to obtain a favourable outcome for his client. This number rose substantially after he became a senior advocate. The first four years by Shri Soli Sorabjee were spent observing and honing the skills required to put convincing arguments before the Judges. Therefore, I learned the importance of perseverance being an important quality to be cultivated in legal career.

Renowned advocate Late Shri Ram Jethmalani, who needs no introduction to the legal world with his career spanning 75 + years in law, stands out as a shining example for law students nationwide. As a lawyer and Professor in Sindh before partition led to the starting of a law firm in Karachi with his friend AK. Brohi, who was senior to him by seven years. In February 1948, when riots broke out in Karachi, he fled to India on the advice of his friend Brohi and came to India with INR 10 in his pocket. The Late Shri Ram Jethmalani fought his first case at 17 in the Court of Sindh under Justice Godfrey Davis, contesting the rule regarding minimum age passed by the Bar Council of Sindh. The first case fought in India as a refugee was against the newly introduced Bombay Refugees Act that treated refugees inhumanely, against which the Late Shri Jethmalani filed a case in the Bombay High Court, praying for the law to be declared unconstitutional, a matter he won.

I studied the golden comments made by the renowned advocate in an independent interview taken back in 2015, that "One should learn to distinguish the profession from a business. One has to always have the notion that the legal profession is a method of service to the public. Law is a profession, the practice of which requires tremendous industry. You must be capable when you are young to put in about 15 to 16 hours of work. Justice does not ultimately depend on law; it depends on facts. And the lawyer must know not only law but a smattering of everything. History, philosophy, science, logic, languages, a lawyer must realize that ultimately advocacy consists in persuading a judge with your oral argument. The more command over language you have, the more persuasive you can be and that puts you ahead of your rivals. A lawyer who only knows the law is a mason; what you need to be is that you should be an architect."

The times have certainly changed, but the lives of legal luminaries will always be a guiding light for all of us to forge our future. My research work enabled me to understand the contours of the Indian Constitution foundational to a law student.

His Lordship reviewing the work done in District and Sessions Court – Bengaluru Rural District after the Court Hours on October 13th [2023]

Chapter 4

Income Tax Event

Meeting at the Office of Principal Chief Commissioner of Income Tax

His Lordship attended the Vigilance Awareness Week at the invitation of the Principal Chief Commissioner of Income Tax, Karnataka and Goa Region, Bengaluru, to deliver a keynote address on 'Corruption Free India for a Developed Nation' as part of the Central Government's sensitisation on reducing corruption in India and for guiding officers of the department. The programme was scheduled at the Cauvery Hall at the Central Revenue Building, Queens Road, Bengaluru.

As an intern, I was allowed to attend the event with His Lordship. The office was a kilometre away, and I decided to walk, not realising that I was supposed to travel in the official car. Following the directions in Google Maps, I arrived at the Income Tax Office. I entered the lift, which unexpectedly stopped on the second floor. As the doors opened, I was startled to hear voices calling my name. I stepped out of the lift, and to my surprise, I was the person His Lordship had asked the officials to guide towards the Principal Commissioner's room. I entered the room to be seated beside His Lordship at the closed-door meeting.

Discussion on the Vigilance Awareness Week

At the office, I shared my new internship beginning in the Chamber of His Lordship before proceeding to the meeting hall for the event. Income tax officials were seated in the audience as His Lordship was formally greeted by the senior

His Lordship and Officials Proceed to the Hall

officials after which the speech began. The speech at the event pertained to the need in enhancing transparency and accountability in reducing corruption by leveraging modern technology. Hon'ble Justice P.S Dinesh Kumar recalled that bribery has been mentioned in ancient texts such as Kautilya's Arthashastra, implying the presence of a centuries-old problem which needs to be tackled responsibly and prudently. His Lordship emphasized on individual integrity in beaconing the principles of honesty in life. The significant role played by the parents in instilling values in children from a young age as part of community-driven efforts was highlighted by His Lordship. The officers were encouraged to work with zeal in performing their duties with utmost devotion and sincerity, to collectively add strength in spearheading the mission of ensuring a corruption-free India for a developed nation, leading to the end of a memorable event.

Chapter 5

Landmark Judgments

Important Judgments

I undertook the voluminous research of His Lordship's Reported Judgments across legal portals and newspapers as part of my internship. After extensive research, I have compiled a few landmark Judgments and news clips to enable a better understanding of important decisions rendered by His Lordship as a Judge and Chief Justice of the Karnataka High Court. The compiled judgments present a fraction of information with the main volume suitable for publication as a book in itself! I sincerely hope that the readers will enjoy the comprehensive reports on few of His Lordship's decisive decisions as you begin to read a chapter which requires considerable time and perseverance to complete with an assurance of a rich learning experience.

Public Sector Banks Permitting Large Exposure Without Adequate Securities a Grave Concern; Revisit Lending Guidelines: Karnataka High Court

16 Feb 2021

The Karnataka High Court has dismissed the petition filed by the founder of NMC Health, Dr Bavaguthu Raghuram Shetty who has challenged the Lookout Circulars (LOCs) issued by Bank of Baroda and Punjab National Bank against him and the endorsement issued by Bureau of Immigration not permitting him to travel to Abu Dhabi. A single bench of Justice P S Dinesh Kumar while dismissing the petitions filed by Shetty said "It is no doubt true that a citizen of this Country has a right to travel. But I hasten to add that persons who take public money have a sacred duty to repay it too."

<u>Court Suggests Lawmakers and Reserve Bank of India to revisit the lending guidelines:</u>

During the hearing the court had called upon the advocates for the Banks to explain on what security the Banks permitted such large exposure (Bank of Baroda Rs 2,000 crore), (Punjab National Bank Rs 800 crore). The answer given was, the Companies to which loans are advanced were 'listed companies' in London Stock Exchange and the share value had shown that the said Companies had high net worth. The court noted "Tangible assets, if any, mortgaged in favour of Banks and their valuation is not forthcoming. If Public Sector Banks are permitting such large exposure without adequate securities, it is a matter of great concern and it shall have serious adverse impact on the economy of this Country. Following which it suggested "It is time, the law makers and Reserve Bank of India re-visit the lending guidelines and the procedures and take necessary remedial measures to ensure that public money is well secured before disbursement."

Court findings:

Justice Kumar went through the Official Memorandum and said that "Clause(c) of paragraph No.7 gives liberty for a person against whom LOC is issued, to approach the officer who has ordered issuance of LOC and explain that it is wrongly issued against him. In the letter written by the Commissioner, Bureau of Immigration, it is stated that the LOCs have been issued at the behest of BOB and PNB. Therefore, the petitioner has to first approach the Bank Authorities. Hence, a direction to provide a copy is unnecessary"

As regards the prayer to declare issuance of LOC without prior notice as illegal and violative Article 14, 19 and 21 of the Constitution of India. The court said "On the face of it, the prayer is misconceived because the whole purpose of issuance of LOC would be defeated by a prior notice. By amending the Official Memorandum, Chairmen of Banks have been empowered to issue LOCs. Bankers may consider issuing LOC to protect the Bank's interest based on the subjective satisfaction of the issuing authority and in this case, the BOB and PNB. Therefore, the argument seeking prior notice is incongruous and therefore rejected."

On considering the prayer made by the petitioner to allow him to travel to Abu Dhabi, the court said "Unless, petitioner exhausts the remedy of approaching BOB and PNB and explains to them as to how the LOCs have been wrongly issued and the Banks pass any further orders thereon, there is no cause of action to consider the said prayer." After perusing the judgments relied by the petitioner and respondents the court said "In the facts of this case, it is relevant to note that petitioner is liable for repayment of about Rs.2800 Crores lent by Public Sector Banks. Undoubtedly, this money belongs to this Country in general and the depositors in particular. This Court cannot lose sight of the fact that money belonging to this Country has been utilized by the petitioner in a foreign country to run his businesses. No material is produced to show that money lent by BOB and PNB has resulted in any development of this country. On the other hand, as on date, it has become a bad debt and public sector banks are fighting litigation in India as also in UAE to recover the same."

It added "Therefore, the reliance in the case of Uco Bank Vs. Dr.Siten Saha Roy is of no avail to the petitioner because the amount involved in the said case was Rs.20 Crores and proceedings were initiated under the SARFAESI Act to recover the amount from the assets mortgaged to the bank." The court opined "In contradistinction, in this case, the amount involved is astronomically high when compared with the Calcutta case, which is about Rs.2800 Crores. It is more than one third of the annual budget of a State like Sikkim. Thus, the amount involved in this case is bound to have serious impact on the economy of this Country and therefore the authorities in the case of Shivashakti Sugars Vs. Renu Sugar Ltd., and Marida Chemicals Vs. Union of India are aptly applicable."

Dismissing the submission that the petitioner is only a guarantor, the court said "In the facts of this case, this admission, without anything more, must entail dismissal of this writ petition because a guarantor is equally liable to repay the debt. Further, it is admitted in the pleadings that petitioner is the promoter of the borrower Companies."

It concluded by saying "In view of the liberty available to the petitioner to approach the Bank authorities and explain that LOCs have been wrongly issued, petitioner is not entitled for relief in these writ petitions."

Karnataka High Court Dismisses Plea Challenging Antrix's Winding Up Proceedings Against Devas with Rs 5 Lakh Cost

30 April 2021

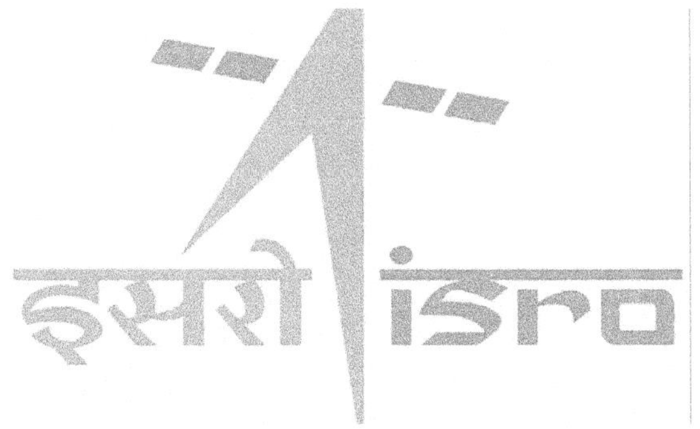

The Karnataka High Court has dismissed a petition which sought to quash proceedings initiated by ISRO-arm Antrix Corporation before NCLT Bengaluru to the wind up Devas Multimedia Private Ltd. The High Court dismissed the petition filed by Devas Employees Mauritius Private Ltd, a shareholder in Devas Multimedia Private Ltd, with a cost of Rs 5 lakhs, after terming it an abuse of process of law. On January 18, the Central Government had authorized Shri. Rakesh Shashibhushan, Chairman-cum-Managing Director of Antrix to present a petition to wind up Devas multimedia on the grounds specified under Section 271(1)(c) of the Companies Act.

Antrix Corporation sought the winding up of Devas Multimedia on the grounds that the Bengaluru-based company's affairs were being conducted in a "fraudulent manner", "the company was formed for fraudulent and unlawful purpose", "the persons concerned in the formation or management of its affairs have been guilty of fraud, misfeasance or misconduct". The High Court bench of Justice P S Dinesh Kumar, while dismissing the petition, agreed with the submission made by the Additional Solicitor General N Venkataraman that 'Registrar' falls in a category as a 'Regulator'. This can also be gathered from the powers and duties of the Registrar of Companies enumerated in Sections 77, 77(2), 78, 81, 83, 93, 137, 157, 206, 208, 209 and 248 of the Companies Act.

The bench also said that "This writ has been filed a day prior to the date fixed for final hearing (Before NCLT), namely March 22, 2021. This amounts to abuse of the process of law and a proxy war on behalf of Devas. Accordingly, it imposed a cost of Rs 5 lakhs on the company which is to be paid to the Registrar General of the court within four weeks.

Court findings:

The bench in its order noted that the petitioner had challenged the order passed by NCLT before NCLAT. The NCLAT had repelled the petitioner's challenge and gave it liberty to join the proceedings in NCLT to raise its objections. Pursuant to the order passed by NCLAT, the petitioner has filed an impleading application in the Company winding up Petition pending before NCLT. Thus, petitioner is privy to all averments contained in the Company Petition.

Further it said "NCLAT has granted liberty to raise all factual and legal pleas before the NCLT. Petitioner has accepted the said order and proceeded further and filed an application under Rules 11 and 34 of the NCLT Rules, 2016 for impleadment in the main petition." It added "Thus, having elected the appropriate forum to oppose the Company petition, this writ has been filed a day prior to the date fixed for final hearing namely March 22, 2021. This amounts to abuse of the process of law and a proxy war on behalf of Devas." The bench opined that "One of the most profound tenets of Constitutionalism is the presumption of Constitutionality assigned to each legislation enacted. Indubitably, Parliament has competence. The sanction accorded by the Central Government does not meet petitioner with any Civil consequence. Devas has not challenged the sanction order."

Accordingly, it held "Petitioner has failed to demonstrate infringement of any rights enshrined in Part-III of Constitution of India. Having held that the Registrar and 'a person authorized by the Central Government' fall into different categories, it does not warrant reading down Section 272(3) of the Companies Act."

'Unwise To Scuttle Investigation': Karnataka High Court Dismisses Amazon & Flipkart Pleas Against CCI Probe'

11 June 2021

The Karnataka High Court on Friday dismissed the writ petitions filed by ecommerce giants Amazon and Flipkart challenging an order passed by the Competition Commission of India for a preliminary investigation into their alleged anti-competitive practices. A single bench of **Justice PS Dinesh Kumar** dismissed the writ petition citing the limitations of the power of judicial review under Article 226 of the Constitution to interfere with a probe ordered by an expert specialized body. "... it would be unwise to prejudge the issues raised by the petitioners in these writ petitions at this stage and scuttle the investigation", the Court said in the judgment.

The impugned order was passed by the CCI in January 2020 under Section 26(1) of the Competition Act directing the Director General to investigate into the allegations against Amazon and Flipkart. The order came on a complaint filed by Delhi Vyapar Mahasangh (an organization of retailers) who alleged that Amazon and Flipkart were giving preferential treatment to a select set of vendors by having indirect control on their operations, especially the launch of smartphones. The DVM alleged that the e-commerce companies were abusing their competitive position. The CCI, finding prima facie merit in the complaint, a probe into the practices of Amazon and Flipkart like discounting practices, exclusive tie-ups and private labels.

Court's findings

The High Court framed three issues:

A. What is the nature of the impugned order passed under Section 26(1) of the Act?
B. Whether a prior notice and opportunity of hearing is mandatory at the stage of issuing direction to the Director General to hold inquiry under Section 26(1) of the Act?
C. Whether impugned order calls for interference?

The issues A and B were answered as:

A. An order under Section 26(1) of the Act passed by the Commission is an 'administrative direction' to one of its wings departmentally and without entering upon any adjudicatory process; and
B. Section 26(1) of the Act does not mention about issuance of any notice to any party before or at the time of formation of

an opinion by the Commission on the basis of information received by it.

The Court observed that that the impugned order showed that the Commission has looked into the information in detail and applied its mind. Under Article 226, the Court cannot substitute the views of the adjudicatory body with its views. Judicial review is not over the decision but over the decision-making process.

"...in a writ petition filed under Article 226 of the Constitution of India, seeking judicial review, the High Court can examine only the decision-making process with the exception namely the cases involving violation of fundamental human rights. The law on the point is fairly well settled", the Court said.

Karnataka High Court Dismisses Challenge to Re-Exam for Police Sub-Inspectors Recruitment

11 Nov 2023

The Karnataka High Court has dismissed a batch of petitions challenging the re-exam for the recruitment of 545 police sub-inspectors. The court has directed the state government to conduct the re-examination through an independent agency, without charging any fresh fee to the candidates. A division bench of Justice P S Dinesh Kumar and Justice T G Shivashakere Gowda dismissed the petitions. It said "The order passed by the State Government, in the facts and circumstances of this case, is just and appropriate and does not call for any interference."

The petitioners had challenged the order of the Karnataka State Administrative Tribunal rejecting their applications. The primary contention raised by the petitioners was that to direct the State Government to segregate the cases of those involved in the malpractice and complete the recruitment process in respect of other candidates. The state government opposed the plea saying the malpractice has taken place in two ways. Firstly, by marking the OMR sheets by obtaining the answers from an outside source using Bluetooth devices. Secondly by tampering with the OMR answer sheets after the examination. It was further submitted that one of the accused persons is the ADGP, Recruitment who was arrested during the course of investigation and remained in jail for some time. The Head of the Recruitment himself being one of the accused, the tampering/manipulation of OMR answer sheets having taken place in his office, the confidence of the general public in the recruitment process has completely eroded, it was argued.

The bench referring to the prosecution case said "Admittedly, the selection is for the disciplined uniformed Police Service who will be entrusted with Law and Order, Crime detection, security etc. Therefore, even if segregation may be remotely possible the same is not worthy of consideration." Noting the admission procedure and the allegations in the case the bench said, "Admittedly, a very senior IPS Officer in the rank of ADGP was the Head of Recruitment Wing. He has been arrested. This clearly indicates that the investigating authority had found prima facie material against the ADGP's culpability."

Rejecting the petitioner's contention that petitioners were prepared for appropriate action including removal, in case they were found guilty of any malpractice; and they were ready to file an affidavit in this Court to that effect it said, "We are not persuaded to accept the said plea because the allegations of malpractice are very grave in nature which include involvement of the Head of the Recruitment Wing, tampering of OMR answer sheets at different levels. The learned Advocate General is right in his submission that trust and confidence upon the Police by the general public is also of paramount importance."

Taking into account that candidates have used Bluetooth devices in the examination hall and some of them were also arrested, the court observed "This leads to a further inference that either the candidates were given early access to the question paper or the question paper was leaked before the examination. Otherwise, it is highly improbable that the external party could relay the answers within time. It is also highly probable that such leaked question papers may have been circulated widely. In such a situation, it is difficult to record a specific finding whether the candidates had early access or the question paper was leaked. But in any event, it is not in dispute that a scam has taken place with the involvement of several persons including an ADGP."

The bench then opined that the evaluation of academic achievement or the suitability of a candidate for public employment necessitates an examination process that adheres to principles of rationality. "Rationality stands as a fundamental requirement within the realm of public administration. The decision to cancel an examination is an extreme step usually taken in the interest of maintaining the integrity of the examination process and to ensure absolute fairness to all the candidates both successful and unsuccessful."

Further the court said that in 2016, the Karnataka State Pre University Board had conducted the examination in Chemistry paper thrice due to paper leakage for the Second PUC students. "Unless a categorical finding is recorded to the effect that there was no malpractice by 'use of Bluetooth', the wisdom of the executive in cancelling the examinations cannot be found fault with. Further, if any finding is recorded with regard to 'use of Bluetooth' by this Court in these proceedings that would amount to pre-judging the issue involved in various criminal trials which exercise cannot be and should not be undertaken in proceedings under Article 226 of the Constitution of India."

Karnataka HC Upholds Non-Renewal of License of G.R. Medical College Due to Deficiencies, Allows Transfer of Enrolled Students to Other Colleges

12 Jan 2024

The Karnataka High Court has dismissed a plea filed by a G.R. Medical College Hospital and Research Centre, Mangalore, challenging the National Medical Council's (NMC) denial of renewal of permission for its 150-1st year MBBS Seats for the academic year 2022-23 and the government's decision to transfer the 150 students to different Medical Colleges in the State. A division bench of Justice P S Dinesh Kumar and Justice T G Shivashankar Gowda dismissed the petition and said "No ground is made out for exercise of extraordinary jurisdiction under Article 226 of the Constitution of India." On 13.12.2021, the college was granted permission by the NMC to establish the

Medical College for an intake of 150 students from the academic year 2021-22. On September 5 & 6, 2022, an inspection was conducted by NMC. Based on the Inspection Report, the renewal of permission has been disapproved for the academic year 2022-23. The bench noted that the inspection was conducted on September 5 & 6, 2022 and no Holiday was declared either two days prior or two days after the inspection. It was observed that the Notification issued by the State Government contained the list of General Holidays sanctioned by the Government for the year 2022, as per which Onam was not declared as a Holiday. No other material is placed on record to establish that there was any holiday declared by the Central or State Governments during the relevant period, the Bench noted.

Thus, it held "Therefore, the Medical College's contention that inspection was contrary to Regulation 8(3)(1) is untenable." In noting that the Medical College had placed on record, the reply dated October 13, 2022, to the show-cause notice, after which a virtual hearing was scheduled and an appearance was made on behalf of the college during the hearing, the bench that reasonable opportunity was provided to the Medical College.

"It is relevant to note that along with the reply to the show cause notice, the College has submitted an explanation with regard to the deficiencies pointed out by the NMC. A careful reading of the same shows that the Medical College has attempted to attribute the deficiencies to the Holiday said to have been declared by the Medical College. Thus, there is no denial of deficiencies," it held. In dismissing the plea, it held that a reasonable opportunity was given to the Medical College and there was no denial about the deficiencies pointed out by the NMC except for an explanation that the Medical College had declared a Holiday on the day of inspection.

The bench also noted that admittedly, 150 students were admitted for 1st year MBBS course for the academic year 2021-22, and the permission for renewal had been disapproved by the NMC for the academic year 2022-23, leaving the students in jeopardy. Thus, the Court allowed the State's action to relocate the candidates to different colleges in the State to enable them to pursue their next academic year.

Junior Court Officer Should Not Be Permitted to Draw Higher Pay Scale to That of Seniors in Solitary Cadre: Karnataka High Court

5 Mar 2024

The Karnataka High Court recently directed the Registrar General of the Court to reconsider the representation made by 12 Court officers, seeking to cure anomaly in their pay scale with regards to Section 6(b) of the High Court of Karnataka (Officers and Officials) Revised Pay Rules, 2018.

A single judge bench of Chief Justice P S Dinesh Kumar (now retired) allowed in part the petition filed by Umashankara C and other and said, "The issue requires to be reconsidered by the 1st respondent, in the light of the judgments of the Apex Court, which clearly depicts that the junior should not be permitted to draw a higher pay scale to that of the seniors in a solitary cadre."The petitioners had approached the court questioning a memo dated 03-092021, by which their joint representation seeking setting right of the anomaly of pay fixation qua the 2nd respondent (S.N. Nataraja) who despite being the junior to the petitioners is given a higher pay scale than that of the petitioners. It was argued that Nataraja, despite being junior to the petitioners, is drawing a higher pay scale. Owing to this disparity in the pay scale, petitioners submitted a representation, which was rejected without them being given an opportunity of being heard.

The bench noted that in terms of the notification dated 06-03-2018 the High Court of Karnataka (Officers and Officials) Revised Pay Rules, 2018 was notified adopting Central Civil Services (Revised Pay) Rules, 2008 and Central Civil Services Pay Rules, 2016 to all the officers of the 1st respondent with effect from 06.10.2004. Then referring to the endorsement issued by the registry taking shelter under Rule 7 r/w Rule 10 of the 6th Central Civil Service (Revised Pay) Rules 2008 and 7th Central Civil Service (Revised Pay) Rules of 2016 to reject the claim of petitioners that they do not fulfil the conditions prescribed in the Rules, the court said, "Rule 7 r/w Note 10 of the Rules 2008 is applicable to a senior Government servant promoted to higher post before 01.01.2006. Petitioners were not promoted to the cadre of Court Officers before 01.01.2006."

Relying on Apex court judgments in the case of Jaipal V. State of Haryana (1988) the court said, "The 1st respondent (Registrar General) has to reconsider the case of the petitioners, strictly in consonance with the judgments rendered by the Apex Court referred to supra not with reference to Rule 7 r/w Note 10 of the Rules 2008." Allowing the petition in part the court set aside the endorsement and remitted the matter for fresh consideration, within three months.

IBM Philippines Not Liable for TDS Under Income Tax Act: Karnataka High Court:

13 Feb 2023

The Karnataka High Court held that IBM Philippines is not liable for TDS under Section 195 of the Income Tax Act, 1961. The Court was dealing with the appeals filed by the Income Tax Department against IBM India Private Limited. A Division Bench of Justice P.S. Dinesh Kumar and Justice T.G. Shivashankare Gowda observed, "the payments received by IBM Philippines shall not be liable for TDS under Section 195 of the IT Act. Therefore, assessee cannot be deemed as an 'assessee in default'." The appeals filed by the Revenue were against the common order passed by the Income Tax Appellate Tribunal (ITAT).

The High Court in view of the facts and circumstances of the case asserted, "IBM Philippines is carrying out the work described in the agreement between IBM India and P&G India. Hence, IBM Philippines was not rendering any technical service and therefore, the income in the hands of IBM Philippines is a business income." The Court answered the questions of law in favour of the assessee and against the Revenue. "The ITAT has, in our considered view rightly recorded in para 8.1.3

of its order that as per Article 7(1) of Indian Philippines DTAA, the business profits of an enterprise of a Contracting State shall be taxable only in that State unless the enterprise carries on business in the other Contracting State through a permanent establishment situated therein. Admittedly, there is no permanent establishment of IBM Philippines in India. As per Article 23 of DTAA, the business profit of IBM Philippines shall be taxable in that State only", said the Court. The Court also noted that the transactions between the assessee and IBM Philippines were in the course of its business and the same has not been disputed by the Revenue. Accordingly, the Court dismissed the appeals.

If Insured Person Is to Exercise Due Diligence Everywhere, Purpose of Insurance Would Fail: Karnataka HC Directs Insurer to Pay NTC

15 Apr 2023

While partly allowing an appeal against the impugned order of the Additional City Civil and Sessions Judge, Bangalore, the Karnataka High Court has directed the United India Insurance Co. Ltd. (the insurer) to pay money to National Textile Corporation (NTC), as per the insurance policy. The Court held that If the insured is expected to exercise diligence everywhere, the entire purpose of insurance would fail. A Division Bench of Justice P.S.

Dinesh Kumar and Justice T.G. Shivashankare Gowda observed, "Generally, a person enters into insurance policies or contracts to protect himself from certain risks or contingencies which cannot be foreseen or taken care of. Diligence has to be exercised wherever possible but if the insured person is expected to exercise diligence everywhere, the question of contingencies or perils would never arise and the entire purpose of insurance would fail.".

The Bench held, "In the present case, NTC is a Government of India undertaking having several branches across the country. It has appointed various depot keepers. It is impractical to expect NTC to verify the genuineness of every bank guarantee and it is for the said reason NTC has taken the Policy. The insurer has covenanted to indemnify the NTC against any loss or damage occurring due to fraud or criminal act on the part of the depot keepers."

The Court also noted that NTC did exercise the necessary due diligence by lodging a complaint against the depot keeper in the jurisdictional police station and further placed reliance on the case of the Apex Court in Suraj Mal Ram Niwas Oil Mills (P) Ltd. Vs. United India Insurance Company and observed - "There is no ambiguity in the conditions of the Policy and if the terms of the policy are strictly construed/interpreted, as held in Suraj Mal, NTC was only required to use due diligence in prosecuting the depot keeper which has been done by lodging a police complaint." The Court also stressed upon a settled position that if there is any ambiguity, the interpretation would fall in favour of the insured person

The Bench further also added that the issuance of a fake bank guarantee by second Defendant is a dishonest act and therefore, covered by the Policy, hence NTC would be entitled to the insurance claim from the insurer. The Court, however, made the insurer liable to a sum of Rs.13 lakhs as opposed to the claim of 25 lakhs.

"A Classic Case of Speculative Litigation Causing Huge Loss of Judicial Time" - Karnataka HC Reverses Specific Performance Judgment Against Trust

3 Oct 2023

The Karnataka High Court has reversed a judgment of specific performance against a trust saying that it is a classic case of speculative litigation causing huge loss of judicial time. An appeal was filed against the judgment and decree passed by the Additional City Civil and Sessions Judge decreeing the suit for specific performance of contract. A Division Bench comprising Justice P.S. Dinesh Kumar and Justice T.G. Shivashankar Gowda held:

"We may record that this is a classic case of speculative litigation causing huge loss of judicial time. The defendant Trust has been compelled to defend its cause for nearly 30 years. Therefore, in our considered view, this appeal deserves to be allowed with exemplary cost."

The High Court noted that "It is first plaintiff's case that he is in physical possession of 168.06 acres. In the cross-examination, it was suggested to him that he was not in the possession of the suit property and he has denied the same, but he has stated that APMC had acquired the property and the possession is with the APMC. Second plaintiff in his examination has stated that he was in the possession of the property from the year 1982." The Court said that though the suit is based on an agreement of the year 1982, the second plaintiff has claimed that he had given the entire sale consideration to Parameshwara. "He has not chosen to enforce the agreement on his own. On the other hand, he has filed an application for impleadment in the year 2004, based on Assignment Deed alleged to have been executed by Parameshwara in 2002. Parameshwara has opposed the application denying the Assignment Deed", further noted the Court.

The Court added that the second plaintiff who claims to be in possession has remained complacent with regard to the transaction which originated in the year 1982 for 22 years. "The instant suit is one for specific performance of 'Agreement to Sell'. The first agreement is not produced. The second agreement is not proved. Payment of consideration is not proved. Parameshwara has admitted that he has not even got a legal notice issued in a sale transaction of 168 acres of land in Bengaluru. The alleged second agreement is of the year 1982 and the instant suit is filed in 1994 after a lapse of 12 years. The suit has been decreed based on learned Trial Judge's 'inference' and 'presumption' and therefore, unsustainable in law", also observed the Court.

NEWS CLIPS:

Levy of Forest Development Fee is Ultra Vires to the Constitution: Karnataka HC –

By Tax scan Team

The High court of Karnataka made a landmark judgment quashing the Forest development fees. The division bench comprising of Chief Justice MR Subhro Kamal Mukherjee and Justice P S Dinesh Kumar were dealing with writ petitions filed by more than 40 mining companies from whom the state of Karnataka has been collecting Forest Development Fee since 2008.

The petitioners unanimously pleaded that there is no quid pro quo in form of a service or benefit for a fee to be levied. Further, they also argued that legislative competence to enact the impugned legislation. The State, on the other hand, argued that the levy is in the nature of 'fee' and not 'tax'. Allowing the petitions, the bench observed that the levy has no constitutional validity since the state government has no right to impose it. After analysing the levies of NPV/CA with Forest Development Fee, the bench noted that the State Government envisages to enhance the forest by using the fee. "NPV and compensatory afforestation charges are collected by the leaseholders to compensate, for the ecological loss and diversion of forest. Therefore, though the object of the State Government is laudable, we are afraid that duplication is unsustainable," the bench said. The bench also ordered for refund of any such fees levied from the aggrieved parties even after a prerequisite prayer by Mr. S.K. Bagaria, the advocate appearing on behalf of the state. Rejecting the State's prayer, the bench ruled that all payments and acceptances were without prejudice to the rights and contentions of the writ petitioners in the pending writ petitions.

BBC, Discovery, Netflix to face contempt for violating interim order –

They also alleged that three persons had pocketed millions of rupees without remitting any amount towards the Tiger Reserve Fund.

Express News Service –

BENGALURU: The High Court of Karnataka on January 8 will frame charges for contempt of court against 10 accused, including BBC (UK), Discovery and Netflix, for airing the film 'Wild Karnataka' or 'India's Wild Karnataka', violating an interim order passed, restraining them from telecasting the film. "We are only considering the prima facie case to direct the accused to answer the charge. The material on record shows that even after the interim order, the footage was in the air, no matter broadcast by whom. To record a precise finding with regard to the involvement of the accused, a trial is necessary.

In our opinion, there is sufficient material on record to frame charges against the accused," a division bench of Justice P S Dinesh Kumar and Justice T G Shivashankare Gowda said, after hearing a civil contempt petition filed by Ravindra N Redkar and Ullash Kumar R K on Thursday, while posting the matter to January 8 for framing of charges. The contempt petition was filed for violating an interim order passed by the court, restraining Sarath Champati, Kalyan Varma, Amoghavarsha, Wild Karnataka and Mudskipper and anyone claiming under or through them from using, publishing, reproducing, broadcasting, telecasting, marketing, selling, distributing, exhibiting or in any way dealing with the film or raw footage captured by Sarath, Kalyan Varma and Amoghavarsha and their team under the MoU dated November 3, 2014, with the Karnataka forest department.

The interim order dated June 29, 2021, was passed after hearing the petition filed by Ravindra N Redkar and Ullash Kumar, contending that though the film was intended to be on a nonprofit basis to promote conservation and for educational purposes, Sarath, Kalyan Varma and Amoghavarsha commercially sold it for profit without the knowledge or approval of the KFD, and the film was distributed in over 100 countries to airlines, broadcasters, networks, channels, streaming partners and theatres.

Karnataka HC upholds land acquisition for KG Layout –

This has come as a big relief for thousands of allottees of sites and land owners waiting for the culmination of litigation pending for adjudication for nearly 16 years.

Karnataka High Court. (File Photo | EPS)
Express News Service Updated on: 23 Feb 2024,

Bengaluru: The Karnataka High Court on Thursday upheld the validity of land acquisition proceedings for the formation of Nadaprabhu Kempegowda Layout spread over 4,000 acres by the Bengaluru Development Authority (BDA). This has come as a big relief for thousands of allottees of sites and land owners waiting for the culmination of litigation pending for adjudication for nearly 16 years.

A division bench of Chief Justice P S Dinesh Kumar and Justice C M Poonacha quashed the order passed by a single judge who had in 2014 quashed the preliminary notification and final notification issued in 2008 and 2010, respectively, by the BDA for the acquisition of the land, after hearing a batch of petitions. The single judge's order dated July 11, 2014, was stayed by the division bench on August 18, 2014, on the appeals filed by the BDA and the development of the layout was going on in undisputed lands, except in around 600 acres which was in dispute. Upholding the notifications by allowing the appeals filed by the BDA against the single judge's order, with certain conditions, the court said it adjudicated the matter to take care of the concern of the allottees of sites and land owners.

The court said the BDA and the state government are required to take care to ensure that the directions issued by the court from time to time are implemented in letter and spirit to serve the purpose of the acquisition of land. Among the conditions, the court permitted the land owners/petitioners (excluding the site owners), who are seeking to drop their lands from the acquisition, to make an application to the BDA along with necessary documents within three months. The BDA should take a decision on this within six months. They sought to drop their lands on the ground that their lands are nursery lands, situated within the green belt, and that the buildings constructed by religious/ charitable trusts and similar adjoining lands have been either left from acquisition or denotified.

For site owners who purchased land in the layouts formed before the land acquisition for Kempegowda Layout, the court asked them to register themselves for allotment of sites with BDA within three months by paying the registration fee. They are exempted from payment of the initial deposit. The court made it clear that till completion of this exercise, either for allotment of sites or for dropping of the lands from the acquisition, the possession of the applicants should not be disturbed and the existing construction should not be demolished by the BDA.

Karnataka HC upholds amendment to Co-op Act –

But rules it is to be effective for elections after disposal of petitions challenging amendment

Karnataka High Court

Express News Service –

Bengaluru : The Karnataka High Court has ruled that the 97th amendment to the Karnataka Cooperative Societies Act, 1959, in the Constitution of India on the eligibility of members of cooperative institutions for voting should be effective after disposal of petitions challenging the amendment.

Justice PS Dinesh Kumar passed the order, dismissing a batch of petitions filed by Venkategowda from Mandya district and several others questioning Section 20(2) (a-iv) and (a-v) of the Act. The court, however, clarified that the prayer made by the petitioners' merits consideration as pursuant to interim orders, members of the societies have participated in the elections and many have won.

If the acts of members are not saved, it will lead to a chaotic situation. It is just and appropriate to accept the prayer made by the petitioners. Amended provisions should be effective for elections to be held after the disposal of these petitions, the court added. It noted that the Governor gave his assent to the Act in 2013, but it was not enforced till 2018. Thereafter, several writ petitions have been filed in the high court which has permitted the members to vote and participate in elections through interim orders.

According to the amendment, members should not have the right to vote if he or she or a representative or a delegate has failed to attend three general meetings of the cooperative institutions out of the last five. A member or a representative who has failed to utilise such minimum service or facilities in a cooperative year as may be specified in the by-laws for three consecutive cooperative years should also not be eligible for voting. Declaring the allotment and transfer of quarters to 10 private individuals by the Karnataka Housing Board (KHB) in Shivamogga, done without following due process of law, as null and void, the Karnataka High Court imposed a cost of Rs 1 lakh on the KHB, payable to the Karnataka State Legal Services Authority. A division bench directed Vinoda Bai and nine others from Hosanagara town in Shivamogga district, to hand over the vacant possession of quarters in question, and vacate the premises within 60 days. If they fail to do so, the KHB should evict them.

LS polls: Karnataka High Court notice to EC on plea to curb use of tech-based platforms to bribe voters –

Four politicians have filed petition seeking changes in laws to curb paperless means of electoral corrupt practices

February 02, 2024 –

THE HINDU BUREAU

The High Court of Karnataka has ordered issue of notice to the Election Commission of India on a PIL petition, which has sought directions to the EC to formulate new guidelines and introduce measures to curb newer and innovative corrupt practices, including bribing voters through gift cards, digital payments, and similar technology-based methods during the ensuing elections to the Lok Sabha and all future elections.

A Division Bench comprising Acting Chief Justice P.S. Dinesh Kumar and Justice T.G. Shivashankar Gowda passed the order on the petition filed by four politicians, who had contested from various constituencies and were defeated in the elections held to the State Legislative Assembly in May last year.

The petitioners are Goutham Gowda M. of Kanakapura, Prasad K.R. of Kumbalagodu, A. Manjunath of Bidadi, and Nikhil Kumar K., son of former Chief Minister H.D. Kumaraswamy. The petitioners had earlier approached the Supreme Court, which had asked them to first approach the High Court for their grievances.

Karnataka High Court asks Advocate General to take up issue of parking of vehicles on footpaths –

January 30, 2024 - Bengaluru –

<u>THE HINDU BUREAU</u>

The High Court of Karnataka on Tuesday orally asked the State Advocate-General to take up with the appropriate authorities the issue of parking of vehicles on footpaths across the city as this menace is resulting in severe hardship for pedestrians.

A Division Bench comprising Acting Chief Justice P.S. Dinesh Kumar and Justice T.G. Shivashankare Gowda pointed out that people park their vehicles on footpaths and even junk vehicles are permanently left on the footpath in many places across the city.

"If something can be done with your intervention, it will be good for the citizens and Bengaluru city," the Bench told A-G Shashi Kiran Shetty.

Executive Chairman of the Karnataka State Legal Services Authority (KSLSA):

Karnataka State Legal Services Authority Hall

A notification issued by the Governor's office stated that the appointment as the Executive Chairman of the Karnataka State Legal Services Authority (KSLSA) will be in effect from November 27. His Lordship discussed the remarkable results of the Lok Adalat during a press conference in the Legal Services Authority Hall of the High Court. The State Legal Services Authority submitted a total compensation amounting to Rs 1569 crore awarded to beneficiaries. More than 25 lakh cases were settled through compromise in the National Lok Adalat held on Saturday, December 9 in various levels of courts across the state. A total of Rs 1,569 crore has been given in the form of compensation. His Lordship, who is also the Executive Chairman of the State Legal Services Authority, spoke at a press conference held in the High Court's Legal Services Authority Hall. On Saturday, a total of 1,022 benches across the state, including three benches of the Karnataka High Court, conducted the Lok Adalat.

High Court judge's surprise check at Bowring Hospital reveals shortage of outpatient registration counters:

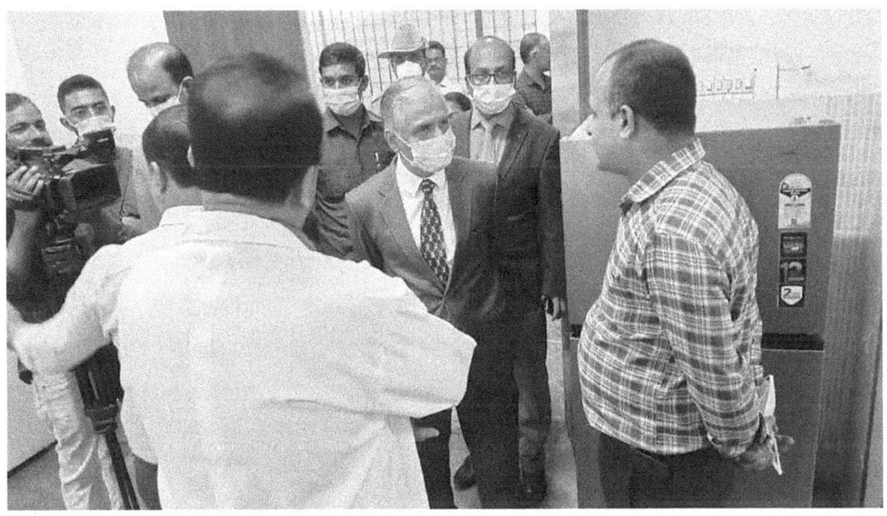

A surprise check at the Bowring Hospital by Justice P S Dinesh Kumar revealed a delay at the outpatient registration counter

Credit: DH Photo/Pushkar Bengaluru: A surprise check of the services at the Bowring Hospital in the city by Justice P S Dinesh Kumar, Judge, High Court of Karnataka and Executive Chairman, Karnataka State Legal Services Authority (KSLSA) on Wednesday revealed a delay at the outpatient registration counter due to very few counters functioning. Arriving at the hospital at 12 pm, the Chairman inspected the hospital's emergency ward and the arrangements made for Covid in the Covid ward. Inspecting the outpatient registration counter, he found very few counters catering to a large group of patients seeking registration.

A few patients complained that they had to wait a long while to complete the registration process, following which, Justice P.S Dinesh Kumar directed the hospital superintendent Dr K Kemparaju to streamline the registration process and open counters as part of a detailed action plan. "Nobody should have to wait for a long time to get registered; anyone coming to the hospital should be attended to at the earliest. Their waiting period must be less than 15 minutes," he told the media, while the superintendent assured that more counters would be opened to cater to more patients. Answering a question about staff shortage at government hospitals, Justice Dinesh Kumar said, "We've to check if there is a staff shortage. If there is, and if we obtain exact figures (of shortage) we will thoroughly check it and submit recommendations to the government". He also directed both the superintendent and the Dean-Director Dr Manoj Kumar to let the KSLSA know what shortcomings the hospital was facing so the authority could intervene, if needed. He also checked the general wards, paediatric wards, neonatal and paediatric ICUs, and the blood collection centre, among other locations, and inquired with the patients about the quality of treatment they were receiving. "I haven't received any complaints from in-patients. I have also seen cleanliness being maintained well in the hospital premises. I have seen the hospital since the 1970s; there has been a marked improvement," he said.

Chapter 6

Yelahanka Air Show

At the Yelahanka Air Force Station to witness the Aero-India 2023

The 14th edition of "Aero India 2023" was held at Yelahanka Air Force Station from the 13th to 17th of February 2023. It had a global media coverage with a combination of major trade exhibitions of the aerospace and defence industries as well as aerial displays by the Indian Air Force.

His Lordship believed that an intern at the office should have a collection of experiences by availing all the opportunities during the internship. I observed members of the Tri-Services and International Guests from the defence sector viewing air show. It gave a surreal experience witnessing advanced jets performing magical moves astounding the audience.

The two-hour air show came to a colourful conclusion as flights together performed symbols of heart and arrow to conclude the event for the day. Flights flew together in two sets to cross over in proximity, giving tense moments to the audience. As we moved out of the Yelahanka Air Base, I knew it was a one-time experience to absorb the atmosphere within the air base.

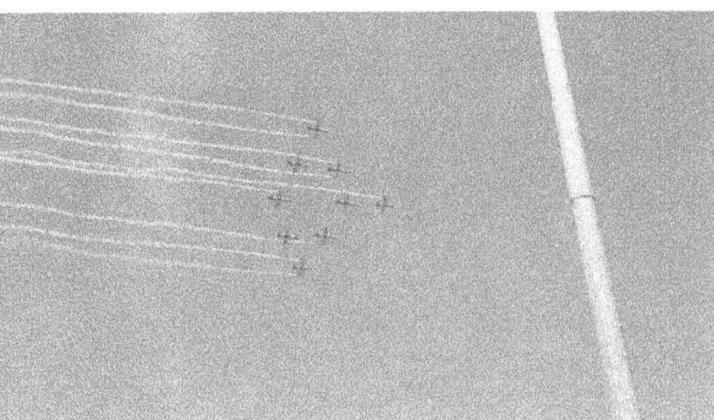

Concluding Performance at the Air Show at Yelahanka Air Force Station

I recalled the words of His Lordship asking me to view the airshow as it may not be possible the next time due to superannuation from the office. My judicial internship was studded with jewels of opportunities beyond legal learning with divine blessings in the Chambers of His Lordship Hon'ble Justice P.S. Dinesh Kumar.

Book Launch

Book Release by Hon'ble Justice P.S Dinesh Kumar

On a busy day at the Karnataka High Court with packed courtrooms, after which there was a line of official meetings and dictation of judgements, I spoke to His Lordship for a few minutes with two requests:

i. A foreword for the book People's Governor, which documents my internship experience at the Office of Lt. Governor Dr. Kiran Bedi, and secondly,

ii. To release the book in my hometown, Namakkal, Tamil Nadu, in the month of September 2023. A quick and powerful reply came from His Lordship in two words: "Why not?". I received the foreword from His Lordship post-midnight on July 12th with blessings for organising the book release.

His Lordship and Hon'ble Dr Kiran Bedi confirmed the travel to Namakkal on September 8th 2023. The book release had to be rescheduled due to an unexpected change in Hon'ble Dr Kiran Bedi's plan because of airspace closure for the G20 Summit. His Lordship encouraged me to re-plan with words of courage and strength, which gave me the confidence to schedule the event on October 7th (Saturday), 2023.

Event at Kailash School of Excellence

On the eve of October 7th 2023, after completing work at the Karnataka High Court, which extended until 8.00 PM, His Lordship began the four-hour and thirty-minute road journey to reach Namakkal at 12.30 AM for the book launch event. The event had 1500 invitees, and newspapers reported it across Tamil Nadu. On October 7th, His Lordship and Hon'ble Dr Kiran Bedi exchanged greetings before the start of the event. As a student, I beamed with pride as Hon'ble Dr Kiran Bedi Madam mentioned that I had moved on from one teacher to the mentorship of His Lordship, who responded by mentioning that my first teacher would always be Dr Kiran Bedi.

Proceeding to the Stage for the Book Release

The event was held at the premises of Kailash School of Excellence, with the school students welcoming His Lordship and Hon'ble Dr Kiran Bedi with "Veera Vanakkam", a traditional art of Silambam in the Tamil culture. The Police Band played the musical rhythm with a group of young children waving the national flag and dancing with ribbons, providing a surreal atmosphere for the school community. The dignitaries planted saplings for a green environment.

Book Released by His Lordship in the presence of School Community

The book release began with the official song and lighting of the lamp, followed by a Welcome Address by the Trustee of the School, Dr Kathirvel. A video documenting the internship experience at the Office of Lt. Governor Dr. Kiran Bedi was played prior to the release of the book by Hon'ble Justice P.S Dinesh Kumar. Dr Kiran Bedi thanked His Lordship for travelling from Bangalore to Namakkal for the book launch and prayed that I emulate the Hon'ble Judge in my lifetime. A short video clip was played before His Lordship's address to the school community. His Lordship noted that the book 'People's Governor' documents a treasured experience in administrative governance at the Office of Lt. Governor Dr Kiran Bedi. His Lordship appreciated the creative design of the cover page and the thoughtful decision to immerse the book with a combination of white and blue to enter the rich world of literature.

Signing of the Book by the Dignitaries

His Lordship Speaks at the Book Launch Event

The foreword incorporated in the book 'People's Governor' extensively covers His Lordship's recorded observations on the book. The foreword read as follows:

"This humble yet striking book is about a young, energetic and smart budding lawyer's experience of his training under the mentorship of the illustrious Dr. Kiran Bedi. At a young age, Mr. Krithik Kailash has added an important feather to his cap of authoring such a credible book. The experiences he has gathered as a mentee is not limited as it gives the reader a chance to understand this young mind's perseverance to learn and excel with such honesty. This book speaks about Dr. Kiran Bedi's life from a tender age when the Indian Police Service made a distinct and positive mark on her mind which led her to become the first woman IPS officer rising to the rank of Director General. Her notable service continued even at the United Nations as an advisor of Police.

The author rightly calls her a 'Global Cop' in this book. This promising officer has not proved her mettle in the Police department as merely a Police officer but also has displayed a humane side by reforming and rehabilitating prisoners at Tihar jail which rendered her the prestigious Ramon Magsasay award.

The author has been fortunate to be guided under the Raj Nivas Youth Engagement Program launched in 2017, an uplifting program for the young minds of the nation. He has keenly spoken about all his learnings under Dr. Kiran Bedi as the Lieutenant Governor of Puducherry highlighting two important aspects. Firstly that 'Raj Nivas'; residence of the Governor, during the tenure of Dr. Kiran Bedi was open to every citizen without any discrimination and secondly that her tenure witnessed a transformation pillared by a mission of accessibility, transparency, and collaboration.

This program has empowered the author in different ways by giving an opportunity to gain theoretical and practical experience by travelling extensively for visioned projects with Dr. Bedi and team such as Mission Green Puducherry, Water Rich Puducherry,

Namme Neer Karaikal, Sitheri Channel Walk and several other outreach programmes. These projects are for the good of the land, nature and humanity at large which are necessary for a sustainable evolution of this world. Conservation of resources, protection of the land, improving the existing eco-system and saving it from contamination in order to pass it on for the future has been strongly taught to these young minds in these programs.

This has become excessively important after the onslaught of a virus called Covid. The timeline now is divided as pre and post Covid era. The author has also brought to the readers as to how Dr. Bedi relentlessly worked during such testing times and offered her services to help the country in this fight against Covid. This program has also opened the doors for the young and brilliant minds to gather significant memories from working for such dedicated causes as well as meeting coveted people of the country which is highly important to broaden one's horizon and to understand life at a deeper level.

The author had a goal-oriented vision that he would reach the gates of Raj Nivas so definitively and he ultimately manifested the same for himself with his hard work and talent. But more importantly, Mr. Krithik Kailash has earned the blessings of Bhagawan Shri Perumal and HanumanJi who have undoubtedly blessed this capable, bright, destined young man to achieve greater success ahead for himself. I also take this opportunity to congratulate the young, bright Mr. Krithik Kailash and pray Bhagawan Shri Krishna to bless him immensely in all his endeavors in life and convey my greetings on authoring his maiden book."

Trustee of the school Mrs Arthy Lakshmi, shared the following in the vote of thanks "Chapter 16 verses - 16.1,16.2, 16.3 of the Bhagavad Gita where Lord Krishna says fearlessness, the perfection of one's existence, cultivation of spiritual knowledge, charity, self-control, the performance of sacrifice, the study of vedic literature, austerity, simplicity, non-violence, truthfulness, freedom from anger- envy, renunciation, tranquillity, aversion to fault finding, compassion for all living entities, gentleness, modesty, steady determination, vigor, forgiveness, fortitude, and passion for honour are the 26 divine qualities endowed in godly citizens. We are blessed to witness this historic book release in the presence of two such godly souls in our life time. As our Thiruvalluvar in his 382nd Kural says:

அஞ்சாமைஈகை அறிவூக்கம்இந்நான்கும்
எஞ்சாமைவேந்தர்க் கியல்பு.

Which means: "Courage, generosity, knowledge (wisdom), motivation (Zeal) are the four essential elements of a successful leader".

The release of the book 'People's Governor' by Hon'ble Justice P.S Dinesh Kumar in the presence of Hon'ble Dr Kiran Bedi has left an everlasting footprint in our quiet city of Namakkal."

Portrait of His Lordship

The portraits of His Lordship and Hon'ble Dr Kiran Bedi, painted by the art teacher, were presented amidst guests who witnessed the historical programme. His Lordship began his return journey to Bangalore after the event by leaving behind historical footprints in the pages of Indian Administration as it was the first time that a Judge of the Constitutional Court released the book of an intern who has documented internship experience in the Office of the Lt. Governor. I considered the event a privileged day where my great teachers blessed a law student to forge a future with strength and determination to lead a purposeful life.

Conclusion of the Event

As the event came to an end, I recollected His Lordship's previous travel to Namakkal on December 27th, 2022, as a surprise visit en route to Srirangam for a brief stop to worship the famous Lord Anjaneya and Narasimhaswamy temple situated at the heart of Namakkal. A temple dedicated to the Goddess Namagiri Lakshmi is located within the temple complex. The great mathematician Srinivasa Ramanujan, whose birthday is celebrated on December 22nd, as the National Mathematics Day in India believed that an equation "had no meaning unless it revealed the mind of god". He prayed to the deity by sitting in the centre of a four-pillared mandapam facing the deity, and it said that he stayed in the precincts of the temple for three days, and Ramanujan got the permission of the Goddess to go to England, in a dream when he was asleep. This is now referred to as the 'Ramanujan Chamber', where His Lordship spent a quiet few minutes before leaving for Srirangam.

*Lord Narasimhaswamy Temple Complex Seated
at the four-pillared Mandapam*

Namakkal's Lord Anjaneya

Tirupati Visit

Group Photo after the Darshan

The Tirupati Balaji temple, known as 'The Temple of Seven Hills', epitomises unwavering faith and spirituality, finding mentions in several aeons-old scriptures and historical texts. His Lordship accepted the request of the Chamber Staff for a visit to Tirupati. On January 12th 2024, we began the five-hour journey with a stop at Sri Sripadaraja Mutt towards the revered Swayambhu Varaha Kshetras, where Lord Venkateswara (Vishnu) is believed to have self-manifested for the welfare of his devotees. The ancient Tirupati temple has witnessed the reigns of many powerful kings over centuries, each leaving their mark on its history. There are about 1180 stone carvings in the temple from different ruling dynasties like the Cholas, Chalukyas, Achchuthan Rayar

Dynasty, and Sadasiva Rayar, each reflecting the artistic and cultural influences of their time. The construction of the Tirupati temple dates back to around 300 AD during the reign of King

His Lordship in the Traditional Attire for the Temple Visit

Thondaiman of Tondaimandalam kingdom, marking the beginning of its rich history. Later, various kings and queens expanded the temple construction and administered the happenings inside the temple complex, adding to its historical significance. For instance, the Pallava

Queen Samavati's donation of her precious jewels and 23 acres of land to the temple, and the Chola Kings' further development of the temple, are notable events in its history. The Vijayanagara rulers, especially Krishnadevaraya, also played a significant role, showering the temple with many ornaments of gold and diamonds.

The Tirupati temple was built skillfully using granites, sandstones, and soapstones. Three Dwarams (doors) lead to the temple Sanctum, with multiple-storied Gopurams (temple towers) on top. The temple's Sanctum Sanctorum (Garbhagriham) is called the Ananda Nilayam, and Lord Venkateswara resides in the Sanctorum facing east. Lord Venkateswara's majestic idol inside the Sanctorum temple stands on the foundation of millions of devotees who visit Balaji every year. On January 13th, the day began with prayers at the Sri Varahaswamy Temple dedicated to the Lord Varaha. Where the legend has it that after saving the earth from the asura Hiranyaksha, Lord Vishnu's Boar Avatar Varaha stayed on this hill on the northern bank of Swami Pushkarini, a sacred pond of immense significance within the main temple complex. The divine darshan of Lord Venkateshwara marked a spiritual culmination of the trip as we began the return journey with a stop at the famous Sri Padmavati temple en route to Bengaluru.

Guard of Honour at Tirumala

Chapter 9

Collegium Resolution

On the 19th of January 2024, I left the court premises early to complete my assigned research work for His Lordship's speech at R.V. College for the following day. In the evening, the Supreme Court Collegium headed by Hon'ble Chief Justice of India Dr.DY.Chandrachud and its members recommended Justice P.S. Dinesh Kumar to be the Chief Justice of Karnataka.

The Supreme Court resolution stated the following:

SUPREME COURT OF INDIA

Re: Appointment of Mr Justice P S Dinesh Kumar, Judge, High Court of Karnataka as its Chief Justice.

The office of the Chief Justice of High Court of Karnataka would be falling vacant consequent upon elevation of Mr Justice Prasanna B Varale to the Supreme Court in terms of our separate recommendation made today. Therefore, appointment to that office is required to be made.

Justice Pratinidhi Srinivasacharya Dinesh Kumar was appointed as a Judge of the High Court of Karnataka on 2 January 2015. He has acquired sufficient experience on the judicial and administrative side as a puisne judge of the High Court. He is due to demit office on superannuation on 24 February 2024 and will have a tenure as a Chief Justice of little over a month. He is endowed with high level of integrity, honesty and competence. He has served the High Court of Karnataka with distinction since his appointment. In view of the fact that Justice P S Dinesh Kumar, as noted above, has a short tenure, in terms of the Memorandum of Procedure, the Collegium resolves to recommend his appointment as the Chief Justice of the High Court of Karnataka, consequent upon the elevation of Mr Justice Prasanna B Varale, Chief Justice of that High Court as a Judge of the Supreme Court.

While recommending his name, the Collegium is well conscious of the fact that in the seniority of Judges of High Court of Karnataka, he is second senior-most Judge after Mr Justice Narendar G who is functioning on transfer in the High Court of Andhra Pradesh and has a long tenure ahead of him.

The Collegium, therefore, resolves to recommend that Mr Justice P S Dinesh Kumar be appointed as the Chief Justice of the High Court of Karnataka consequent upon elevation of Mr Justice Prasanna B Varale to the Supreme Court.

(Dhananjaya Y Chandrachud), CJI
(Sanjiv Khanna), J
(B R Gavai), J

<u>19 January 2024.</u>

The news media widely reported the recommendation by the Supreme Court Collegium. It marked the culmination of a lifetime's hard work and dedication to pioneer the pursuit of justice by His Lordship.

Supreme Court Collegium recommends appointment of Justice P.S Dinesh Kumar as Chief Justice of Karnataka High Court: "In a Resolution passed by the Supreme Court Collegium on 19-1-2024, the name of Justice PS Dinesh Kumar was recommended to be appointed as the 34th Chief Justice of Karnataka High Court. While recommending Justice Dinesh Kumar's name, the Collegium observed that he has been endowed with high level of integrity, honesty and competence and has served the High Court of Karnataka with distinction since his appointment."

I pondered over the scheduled lectures at R.V. College for the Teacher's Conclave. I received the travel confirmation to R.V. College by his Lordship, an event which came with great joy amidst the news of the Supreme Court Collegiums' resolution.

Southern Region Law Teachers Conclave

On 20-1-2024, His Lordship inaugurated the Southern Region Law Teachers Conclave 2023-24 on the theme 'Empowering Legal Educators for tomorrow'. Hon'ble Justice P.S Dinesh Kumar stressed the need for legal educators to undergo training on the implications of cyber law and related legislation to ensure that they remain at the forefront of evolving educational methodologies that incorporate technology. Referring to the rapid technological changes in the next ten years His Lordship emphasized the need for law teachers to be abreast of the latest developments and equip students.

Justice Dinesh Kumar spoke of the evolving nature of legal education by contrasting the methods employed by practitioners and scholars over different generations. His Lordship pointed out that observation and assistance under senior lawyers were no longer the sole source of learning and growth for the current crop of legal professionals. With the exponential increase in access to data and information, Justice Kumar highlighted the need for legal professionals to prepare for an imminent overhaul of the system in the next decade. His Lordship also referred to the paradigm shift that legal education has undergone since the 1990s with the introduction of five-year integrated law programmes.

Conclave Panel

The Conclave consisted of panel discussions and insights from around 20 eminent speakers across various law schools from the South India. The discussions largely focused on the need for a blend of industry and academia to prepare students for the challenges of the professional world. The scope of technology in all aspects of learning with the evolving landscape in preparing the law teachers for increasing competition and globalization was also emphasized. The sessions covered various dimensions of the challenges that the law teachers need to grapple In the 21st century and mechanisms to cope up with the pace and the need for thorough introspection on an individual basis and leadership roles. The sessions also underscored the need for a renewed focus on inclusive education and furthering strong foundational and language skills

After the completion of the event, we proceeded to the High Court. The Registrars and other senior officers welcomed the Chief Justice

Designate. His Lordship's Office was filled with bouquets, shawls and never-ending congratulatory phone calls.

On the 21st of January, Hon'ble Justice P.S Dinesh Kumar participated in the 14th National Conference on enhancing judicial administration which focuses on the application of procedural law and ensuring access to justice at Christ University.

XIV National Conference on Enhancing Judicial Administration: Application of Procedural Law and Ensuring Access to Justice in India

His Lordship recalled that the judicial administration through the application of procedural law has been a continuing process in ensuring a fair and consistent application by ensuring a structured mechanism in the filing of cases for any legal proceeding.

Hon'ble Justice P.S Dinesh Kumar spoke extensively on Civil procedural laws and Criminal procedural laws along with various anecdotes on the alternative dispute mechanisms available to enhance access to justice. The event came to a fruitful end with His Lordship encouraging the students to pursue the path of excellence and service in life.

Chapter 10

Acting Chief Justice

Justice P.S Dinesh Kumar appointed Acting Chief Justice of Karnataka High Court.

The Central Government notified the appointment of Justice P.S Dinesh Kumar as Acting Chief Justice of the Karnataka High Court on January 24th, 2024. The order of appointment notified by Department of Justice read as follows:

Dated : 24th January, 2024.

<u>NOTIFICATION</u>

In exercise of the powers conferred by Article 223 of the Constitution of India, the President is pleased to appoint Shri Justice P. S. Dinesh Kumar, Judge of the Karnataka High Court, to perform the duties of the office of the Chief Justice of that High Court with effect from the date Shri Justice Prasanna B Varale relinquishes the charge of Chief Justice of Karnataka High Court consequent upon his elevation as a Judge of the Supreme Court of India.

(Narayan Prasad) 24.01.2024
Deputy Secretary to the Government of India
Tele : 011-23072149

The Acting Chief Justice Shri P.S. Dinesh Kumar and Senior Judges of the Karnataka High Court travelled to the Kempe Gowda International Airport to bid farewell to Justice Prasanna B Varale, elevated as a Judge of the Apex Court. I witnessed a transition of the high constitutional office. His Lordship travelled from the Airport to the residence of Former Chief Justice of India Sri M.N. Venkatachalaiah to seek the blessings of the renowned jurist.

A Picture with Justice Prasanna.B. Varale at the Kempegowda Airport

His Lordship with Former Chief Justice of India Shri.MN Venkatachalaiah

I had the golden opportunity to introduce myself and converse with Justice MN Venkatachalaiah. Justice M.N. Venkatachalaiah congratulated His Lordship on the elevation as Acting Chief Justice and beamed with pride while speaking with His Lordship.

Justice M.N. Venkatachalaiah wished me great success in my legal journey and posed a question on the revolutionary change which the judiciary will witness in the next decade. I answered by focusing on the role of technology in the landscape of our justice delivery system. My meeting with the 25th Chief Justice of India remains one of the most precious moments in my internship experience. Notably, His Lordship has known Justice M.N Venkatachalaiah for over four decades. The role of Justice M.N. Venkatachalaiah has been pivotal in the successful legal journey of His Lordship.

My First Meeting with the Renowned Jurist

Diamond Jubilee Celebration of Indian Supreme Court commenced in the presence of Hon'ble Prime Minister of India Shri Narendra Modi, Hon'ble Chief Justice of India Dr.DY Chandrachud and Chief Justices of High Court on January 28th - 2024.

Chapter 11

Republic Day

Floral Tributes to National Leaders

His Lordship unfurled the national flag in the Karnataka High Court and Karnataka State Legal Services Authority on the 26th of January 2024, marking the Republic Day function. The Judges of the Karnataka High Court, Members of the Advocates' Association, Staff of the High Court and other invitees were seated at the venue. His Lordship received the guard of honour and paid floral tributes to the portraits of Mahatma Gandhi and Dr B.R. Ambedkar. The Registrar General and Superintendent of Police escorted the Acting Chief Justice to the Flag Post. This was followed by the unfurling of the National Flag and playing the National Anthem. The Police Band staff gave a salute to His Lordship and sought permission from the Acting Chief Justice for dispersal.

His Lordship's Republic Day message was a poignant reflection on the theme chosen for the celebration of India's 75th Republic India - Mother of Democracy and Viksit Bharat'. The speech delved into the historical past of our democratic ethos, highlighting the monumental contributions of the 389 prominent members of the Constituent Assembly.

Speech at the Karnataka High Court

The speech gave a thought-provoking insight into the transformative power of the Indian Constitution, a document that has shaped the social, economic, and political life of Indian society.

"The Constituent Assembly, which first met on December 9, 1946, took precisely two years, 11 months, and 18 days to come up with the final draft. A fine document, handwritten in 1,17,369 words in the English version by the renowned Prem Narain in Italic style and following the best calligraphic tradition of our country. An astonishing fact is that he used 254 pen-holder nibs and devoted six months to complete the writing. Artists from Shantiniketan, including Beohar Rammanohar Sinha and Nandalal Bose, uniquely decorated each page of the Constitution. The original copies of the Indian Constitution were written in Hindi and English. Each member of the Constituent Assembly that drafted the Constitution signed two copies, one in Hindi and the other in English". His Lordship recollected the speech delivered by Independent India's first President, Dr Rajendra Prasad, who observed that they had been able, on the whole, to draft a good Constitution which he trusted would serve the country well. He added, "If the people who are elected are capable and men of character and integrity, they would be able to make the best even of a defective constitution. If they are lacking in these, the Constitution cannot help the country. After all, a constitution like a machine is a lifeless thing. It acquires life because of men who control it and operate it, and India needs today nothing more than a set of honest men who will have the interest of the country before them.

His Lordship spoke on our Constitution's most remarkable feature: Its philosophy Is everlasting, but its structure and clauses are flexible. It contains all the features of a federation, such as two governments, division of powers, written Constitution, the supremacy of the Constitution, the rigidity of the Constitution, independent judiciary and bicameralism. However, the Indian Constitution also contains a large number of unitary features, such as a Strong Centre, a Single

Constitution, the Appointment of a State Governor by the Centre, All India Services and an Integrated Judiciary. His Lordship believed that three things build a nation. The first is noble ideals. The second is the capability of the citizens to achieve these ideals. The third and most significant is each citizen's constant and relentless effort to strive for excellence and take his country forward. The speech concluded by renewing a pledge to achieve the vision of a 'Developed India' by dedicating ourselves to the service of Mother Bharat, leading to the eventful conclusion of the nation's 75th Republic Day celebrations at the Karnataka High Court.

Address to the Members of the Bar

After the Republic Day Message, an event was organized at the Advocates Association within the court complex. The Republic Day celebration marked a unique moment in my internship experience. I travelled with the Acting Chief Justice, Shri P.S Dinesh Kumar, to the Karnataka State Legal Services Authority Office and the High Court.

Celebration of Republic Day at the Karnataka State Legal Services Authority:

Portraits of Mahatma Gandhi and Dr.BR.Ambedkar

The atmosphere was filled with patriotic fervour and celebration to mark the enactment of the Indian Constitution, which has shaped the destiny of a nation governed by the sacred principles of upholding the rule of law and access to justice for all.

Felicitation at the Advocate's Association Hall

On 28 January 2024, the Chief Justice of India, Dr D Y Chandrachud chaired a Ceremonial Bench with Supreme Court Judges and the Chief Justices of 25 High Courts across the country to commemorate the first sitting of the Supreme Court

Ceremonial Bench: On 28 January 2024, the Supreme Court of India celebrated the Foundation Day and commenced the Diamond Jubilee year of its inception. The historical occasion saw the Chief Justices of the 25 High Courts seated in Court Hall – 1 of the Supreme Court along with the Apex Court Judges. This significant moment in history marked His Lordship attending the momentous gathering amidst the presence of the distinguished functionaries.

The Supreme Court Chronicle carried the following report: "Commemorating the First Sitting of the Supreme Court Over the span of seventy-five years since its inception, the Supreme Court has undergone profound transformations, both in its structure and in the legal framework within which it operates. From a modest beginning with six Judges, it has now expanded to a formidable strength of thirty-four."

Chapter 12

Chief Justice of Karnataka

Governor of Karnataka Shri. Thawar Chand Gehlot felicitates Chief Justice P.S Dinesh Kumar on the 3rd of February – 2024

On 31st January 2024, the Hon'ble President of India issued the warrant of appointment to Justice P.S. Dinesh Kumar as the Chief Justice of Karnataka. The swearing-in ceremony was fixed on 3rd February 2024 at 10:30 AM. The notification on 31st January 2024 came late in the evening. After a long day of work in the court, Justice P.S. Dinesh Kumar stopped at the MTR, a popular chain of restaurants, for a cup of coffee. I was present with Mr. Vinayak, a devoted walk enthusiast at Lalbagh.

Picture taken After the Notification as Chief Justice

As the much-awaited notification came, we clicked a picture to document the moment which came after 34 years of hard work and dedication to the legal profession as an eminent advocate and a distinguished Judge. The preparation for the swearing-in ceremony began in full swing as the wheel of time spun for Justice PS Dinesh Kumar to be appointed as the 34th Chief Justice of Karnataka.

On 1st February 2024, upon the news of notification as the Chief Justice of Karnataka, His Lordship travelled to meet Hon'ble Justice Shivaraj V Patil, Former Judge, Supreme Court of India, in whose chambers Justice PS Dinesh Kumar began to work as an advocate. His Lordship described the meeting as his 'best moment' in life. Justice Shivaraj V Patil beamed with happiness and pride to witness the rise of his student as the Chief Justice of Karnataka. In the forty–five–minute meeting, Justice Shivaraj V Patil quipped that 'positions and possessions change, but relationships must be permanent and everlasting in nature.'

Meeting with Justice Shivaraj V Patil

Felicitation by Justice Shivaraj V Patil

His Lordship had attended the book release of Justice Shivraj V Patil's Autobiography titled Time Spent and Distance Travelled. Justice Patil mentions his journey to reach the land's highest constitutional court in this book. Justice Patil gifted a signed copy of the book received by Justice PS Dinesh Kumar with utmost reverence and gratitude. His Lordship was sworn in as the 34th Chief Justice of Karnataka at the Karnataka Raj Bhavan's Glass House on 3rd February 2024 at 10.30 AM. My family and I were seated at the venue an hour before the ceremony. Traditional band tunes were played upon the arrival of His Excellency The Governor of Karnataka for the oath ceremony. The grand and splendid event witnessed a large audience who gave thunderous applause as Justice P.S Dinesh Kumar arose to take oath as the Chief Justice.

Justice P.S. Dinesh Kumar taking oath as Chief Justice of Karnataka High Court, at Raj Bhavan in Bengaluru, in the presence of Governor Thawar Chand Gehlot and Chief Minister Siddaramaiah on February 3, 2024.

His Lordship read the following:

"I, Pratinidhi Srinivasacharya Dinesh Kumar, having been appointed Chief Justice of the High Court of Karnataka, Bengaluru, do swear in the name of God. I will bear true faith and allegiance to the Constitution of India as by law established. I will uphold the sovereignty and integrity of India. I will duly and faithfully, to the best of my ability, knowledge and judgment, perform the duties of my office without fear or favour, affection or ill will and that, I will uphold the Constitution and the laws."

I cherished each moment of my second visit to the Karnataka Raj Bhavan, home to the Governor of Karnataka. It has a rich history of over 180 years, with various art collections and an exquisite garden spread across sixteen acres.

Picture at the Karnataka Raj Bhavan

Nearly a year ago, The President of India notified the appointment of two Additional Judges to the Karnataka High Court, and the swearing-in ceremonies of the Judges were scheduled at the Karnataka Raj Bhavan.

His Lordship granted the law clerks and me permission to attend the event. His Lordship ensured that we were seated at a visible space before proceeding to the seats reserved for Hon'ble Judges.

First Visit to Karnataka Raj Bhavan

The decision to permit us to attend the swearing-in ceremony marked a significant day in my internship experience. A year had passed with the revolving wheel of time. I left the premises towards the official chamber of the Chief Justice along with my parents and sister. His Lordship acknowledged my family members who had the opportunity to converse with the Hon'ble Chief Justice on an occasion that happens but rarely in history as we were fortunate to be part of one such event where Guru Shri P.S Dinesh Kumar became the head of Karnataka Judiciary.

On the 5th of February 2024, His Lordship was formally welcomed at the Chief Justice's Courtroom by the Advocates' Association, Bengaluru. The Reply Speech delivered by Hon'ble Chief Justice Shri P.S Dinesh Kumar read as follows:

"Mr. Chairman,

I am grateful for the kind words you have spoken of me. The Bar and Bench represent the wheels of a chariot involved in dispensing justice. Erudite Judges and fine advocates have shaped the constitutional framework of our land. I recollect the contribution of my esteemed colleagues who have walked this path before me, leaving an indelible mark on the rich legacy of legal history in Karnataka.

The judiciary plays a fundamental role in shaping the foundations of a just society built upon the rule of law and the pursuit of justice for all. The concept of 'dharma' has evolved over centuries to be fortified with the enactment of the Indian Constitution. The evolving nature of law and a dynamic socio-economic landscape necessitates a judiciary that is resolute in its commitment to justice. As the Chief Justice, it shall be my earnest endeavour to maintain the highest traditions of this court.

The technological revolution has ushered in a change in the entire justice delivery system. The initiative of e-Court has led to the introduction of paperless courts where no paper is used, from the initial presentation of case papers to its disposal and archival. Computerizing active case files and a database to track a case from the time it is registered till it is disposed of has enabled easy search, retrieval, grouping, information processing, judicial record processing, and the disposal of cases. Videoconferencing options to appear in Courts have saved considerable costs and time in delivering justice.

Karnataka High Court is pioneering to improve the Information and Communication Technology [ICT] in the judicial system. We have taken numerous innovative steps to revolutionize our justice delivery system. Increasing the number of judicial officers fully equipped to tackle cases involving specialized knowledge of the law is crucial in saving time and delivering justice to litigants.

Dispute resolution through Lok Adalats and other alternative dispute mechanisms such as Arbitration and Mediation is yielding positive results and responses. Our quest is to achieve the vision of a welfare state committed to securing justice, liberty, and equality for the people, ultimately promoting the fraternity and dignity of the individual. We must participate actively by assuming responsibilities, and coming forward to give the best for our legal profession.

I am deeply indebted to the Almighty for bestowing this high position in my life. The 47th Shloka of 2nd Chapter in Bhagavad Gita teaches us that 'one has a right to work but never to its fruits. Let not the fruits of action be your motive, nor let your attachment be to inaction.

I take this opportunity to place on record my gratitude to Hon'ble Dr. Justice D.Y. Chandrachud, Chief Justice of India, Hon'ble Mr. Justice Sanjiv Khanna and Hon'ble Mr Justice B. R. Gavai, Judges of the Supreme Court of India, for reposing confidence in me and recommending my name for Chief Justiceship.

I am grateful to my senior Hon'ble Mr Justice Shivaraj Patil, Former Judge, Supreme Court of India, Hon'ble Justice M. N Venkatachalaiah, Former Chief Justice of India, Hon'ble Justice HL Dattu, Former Chief Justice of India, Mr Soli Sorabjee, Former Attorney General of India and several other seniors who have guided and supported me throughout.

On this occasion, please permit me to remember with reverence my pious mother and father the late Shri. Pratinidhi Srinivasacharya, whose life as a Judge embodied intellectual prowess and divine faith. I express my gratitude to my Gurus, family members, and friends who have extended their unconditional support to me throughout."

The customary speech officially marked the first day as the Chief Justice before presiding over the listed cases. As the Chief Justice, His lordship heard over a hundred and ten matters daily. His Lordship spearheaded the mission to reduce the pendency of cases. I could follow the same work pattern followed by His Lordship in disposing of the cases. Advocates needed to be well prepared with the facts of their cases and nuances of law. Pointed questions by the Bench revolved around multifaceted contours that required rich legal understanding and a grasp of the law. Junior counsels were appreciated for striving to present their case with the court's wisdom enabling them to improve their confidence and ability to argue matters. As an intern, I keenly noted the arguments and researched various questions of law. His Lordship had a packed schedule over the weekend as part of the official visits and inauguration of projects which is elucidated in the forthcoming chapters.

Left to Right: Sister K Deeksha, Mother Mrs. Arthy Lakshmi, Father Dr. Kathirvel, Myself, His Lordship, Respected Jayashree Madam in the Official Chamber of the Chief Justice after the Swearing - in – Ceremony.

Chapter 13

Official Visit

Felicitation by the Principal District and Sessions Judge Shri Shantaveer Shivappa and Judicial Officers in Udupi on 9th of February – 2024

The Hon'ble Chief Justice of Karnataka Shri P.S Dinesh Kumar was scheduled to officially visit the following places on February 10th and February 11th 2024. The travel plan covered the cities of Mangalore, Udupi, Sagar, Shikaripura and Mathur en route to Bangalore. On February 9th, 2024, I began the six-hour road journey towards Mangaluru Airport with a refreshment break in the city. His Lordship and the official entourage of the Chief Justice arrived at the Mangaluru Airport. We travelled to Udupi by covering sixty – kilometres by road for a stay in a city which is dear to His Lordship, whose connect with the temple land is more than fifty years of regular travel to worship Sri Krishna Matha.

The Principal District and Sessions Judge Shri Shantaveer Shivappa and judicial officers received His Lordship whose travel marked the first official visit after taking oath as the Chief Justice of Karnataka. We offered prayers in the Udupi Sri Krishna Temple, founded by the Vaishnavaite Saint Sri Madhavacharya in the 13th Century. On February 10th, 2024, the day began by visiting Sri Durgadevi Temple, Kunjaragiri and Pajaka Kshetra, which is the birthplace of revered Vaishnavaite Saint Sri Madhavacharya, the founder of Dvaita philosophy and Sri Krishna Mutt.

Picture in the premises of the Sri Durgadevi Temple, Kunjaragiri

Group Photo with His Lordship

We travelled back to the Guest House as the official events were scheduled to begin for the day. The Udupi Bar Association organized a state-level cultural fest for the advocate community at Udupi Court premises. His Lordship spoke about the yesteryears of travel to Udupi and the various facets of work undertaken by the Karnataka High Court to enable and enhance litigants' access to justice.

Lighting of the Lamp at the Udupi Bar Association

Speech at the Udupi Bar Association

Felicitation After the Inauguration of State Level cultural Fest in Udupi

After the event, the Udupi Bar Association felicitated His Lordship and Respected Jayashree Madam. We returned to the Udupi Guest House for lunch and headed towards Mangaluru for the next event.

Hon'ble Chief Justice Shri P.S Dinesh Kumar inaugurated the newly constructed Judicial Officers Quarters Mangaluru, Dakshina Kannada, at 2 PM. The District Judiciary, Dakshina Kannada and Public Works Department jointly organized the inaugural function.

Event at District Judiciary – Mangaluru

Addressing the Members of District Judiciary

After the event, we headed towards the District Court Complex as His Lordship was scheduled to address the Judges. The official visit to the District Court Complex, Mangaluru, is vivid in my memories. His Lordship instructed the staff to unlock a hundred-year-old courtroom. I witnessed the discussion and instruction given by His Lordship to revamp the room and put it to use at the earliest possible time. This will help to increase the availability of space and courtrooms in the court complex, which is foundational to the Judicial Branch of Government.

Felicitation after the Event

En route to Kollur Mookambika Temple

The journey from Mangaluru towards Sagara covered two hundred kilometres with a stop at the most ancient Kollur Mookambika Temple. The temple visit was a surprise plan enroute to Sagara with a darshan of Shri Mookambika Devi. We reached Sagara at 8.30 PM for the night's stay at the Guest House. The visit to Shri Shridhara Swami Ashram located in the village of Varadahalli, with the climb up the famous hill shrine, marked the spiritual plane of the visit. His Lordship gracefully accepted the request to have food at the Ashram until departure from Sagara.

Planting of Sapling in Sagara on the 11th of February

Member of Shri Shridhara Swami Ashram Speaks to His Lordship

The official events began with the Guard of Honour and the newly constructed 'Vakeelara Bhavana' inaugural function. This was followed by a program organized by the Sagara Bar Association in the presence of Justice R Devdas and other eminent dignitaries. The Executive Committee Members were present for the event.

His Lordship's Address After the Inauguration of 'Vakeelara Bhavana'

Hon'ble Chief Justice of Karnataka, Shri P.S Dinesh Kumar, spoke about the mission to expand judicial infrastructure and other facilities for the welfare of the advocate community. The organizers felicitated Hon'ble Chief Justice and awards were presented to the members of the District Judiciary and Public Works Department by His Lordship before the conclusion of the event.

Inaugural Function of the Newly Constructed Judicial Officers Quarters at Shikaripura

Judicial Officers Quarters

The next official event was the inaugural function of the newly constructed Judicial Officers Quarters at Shikaripura. A forty-five-minute road journey to attend the event and address the members of the District Judiciary. A customary photograph followed the event. This marked the return journey towards Bengaluru. During the return journey, Hon'ble Chief Justice briefly stopped at the Mathur Village, which has a hundred per cent Sanskrit-speaking population. The traditional reception with chanting of hymns and shlokas followed by a meeting with villagers through a unique session connected us with the rich traditions and history of the land in the memorable journey to Bangalore.

Stop at Mathur Village enroute to Bengaluru

Addressing the Village Members

Departure from Mathur after an Eventful Session

The two-day official visit of the Hon'ble Chief Justice of Karnataka, Shri.P. S Dinesh Kumar, is now etched in the history of Karnataka Judiciary. I was fortunate to be part of the historical visit. A combination of legal and spiritual learning enhanced my knowledge about the functioning of the Indian Judiciary. The Official Visit continued the following days. On February 12th, His Lordship, after a busy day at the Court, travelled to Devananahlli to attend a programme arranged by the Bar Association and to unveil the portrait of Swami Vivekananda at Shidlaghatta. Hon'ble Chief Justice verified the daily orders and Judgments en route the travel to save valuable time, whereas I had the duty to proof-read the same to ensure hassle-free grammar, providing a surreal travel experience with His Lordship.

Work enroute to Devanahalli on 12th of February

Speech after unveiling the portrait of Swami Vivekananda at Siddleghutta

The legal fraternity warmly welcomed the Hon'ble Chief Justice in Devanahalli, where His Lordship addressed the members in the home language, giving a personal connection to the event. Members of the Bar recalled the historical oath ceremony of His Lordship as the second person to hold the position from the same Parent High Court. His Lordship shared various anecdotes on the life of Swami Vivekananda after unveiling the portrait at Siddleghutta and felicitated the advocate community. A remarkable internship experience added colours to my rich learnings as the events for the day concluded.

Right to Left: His Lordship, Grandfather Sivam, Grandmother Shakuntala Sivam, Mother Mrs.Arthy Lakshmi and Myself.

Travel to Mysore

STAR OF MYSORE

Karnataka Chief Justice to Visit City This Evening

Hon'ble Chief Justice Shri P.S Dinesh Kumar travelled to the New Court Complex Malalavadi, Mysuru. His Lordship inaugurated the Mysuru Judicial Employees Building and two additional lift facilities at Mysuru District Court Complex. I had the opportunity to witness the inauguration of the "CCTV surveillance system' in the venue. His Lordship also inaugurated the upgraded library of Mysore Bar Association and virtually inaugurated Judicial officers' Quarters at Hunsur and Periyapatna constructed at an estimated cost of Rs. 1 crore each. Hon'ble Chief Justice unveiled a plaque featuring the Preamble of the Constitution The event was jointly organized by the Mysuru District Legal Department, the Public Works Department and the Mysuru Bar Association.

Karnataka High Court Judges Justice K. Somashekar, Justice Srinivas Harishkumar, Justice T.G. Shivashankaregowda were present at the event.

Justice P.S. Dinesh Kumar inaugurates upgraded library of Mysore Bar Association and Judicial Officers' Quarters at Hunsur & Periyapatna

The Chief Justice of Karnataka urged young lawyers to integrate ethical principles into their professional responsibilities and personal lives. His Lordship underscored the significance of upholding discipline, ethical conduct and thorough preparation while carrying out their duties. The Chief Justice encouraged young advocates to meticulously prepare for their Court appearances.

Emphasising the importance of maintaining integrity and moral values, His Lordship advised aspiring lawyers to approach their work with diligence and commitment to justice. His Lordship stressed the need for thorough research of relevant case laws and underscored the paramountcy of faith and moral principles in legal practice.

Upgraded Library of Mysore Bar Association

Unveiling the Inaugural Stone of the Judicial Officer's Quarters at Hunsuru and Periyapatna.

The Chief Justice shared his own experience as an advocate, recalling instances where he prioritised honesty by admitting to the Court when he was unprepared for arguments. Reflecting on his journey as a judge spanning over three decades, His Lordship expressed humility in assuming the role of Chief Justice. His Lordship recollected about his father's tenure as a district judge in Mandya during 1969-70 and drew inspiration from dignified figures like Dr. H. Narasimhaiah, former Vice-Chancellor of Bangalore University, known for his integrity and simplicity. The Chief Justice recounted Dr. Narasimhaiah' s influence on his academic choices and expressed his commitment to emulate such noble individuals by upholding simplicity and integrity.

Guard of Honour at the New Court Complex Mululuvadi, Mysuru

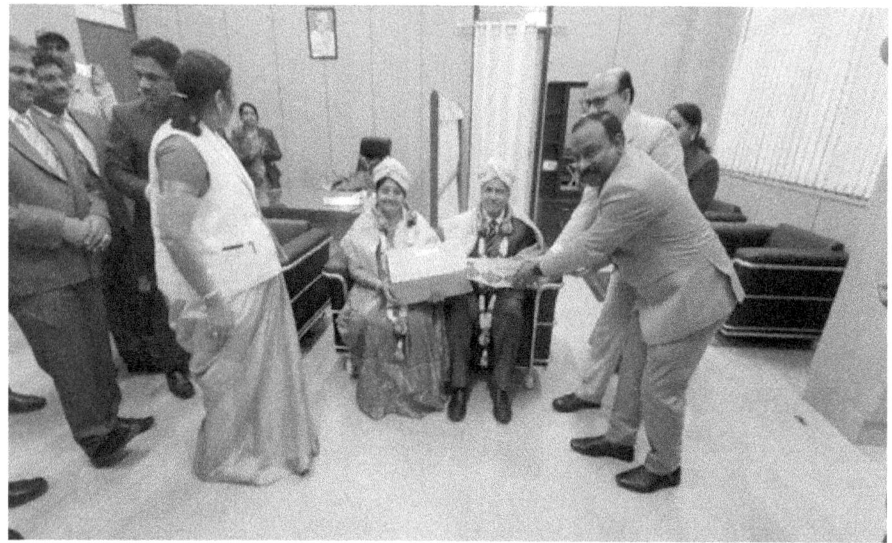

Felicitation at the District Court Complex – Mysore

Conclusion of the Event

I recollected my previous visit to Mysore with His Lordship who addressed the students of JSS Law College, inspected the work of District Judiciary and addressed the members of Mysore Bar Association to mark the first half of the schedule. His Lordship's speech in the College pertained to the marking of 'Constitution Day'. His Lordship noted the words of a member of the Constituent Assembly, H.V. Kamath, who once commented, "The emblem and the crest that we have selected for our assembly is an elephant. It is perhaps in consonance that our Constitution, too, is the bulkiest that the world has produced.". A single Constitution for both the Centre and the States changed the landscape of administrative governance.

His Lordship enumerated the six Fundamental rights enshrined in the Indian Constitution and guaranteed to all citizens. Articles 12-35 of the Indian Constitution dealing with Fundamental Rights. These human rights are conferred upon the citizens of India, for the Constitution is clear that these rights are inviolable. The six fundamental rights of the Indian Constitution are:

a] Right to Equality (Article 14-18) guarantees equal rights for everyone, irrespective of religion, gender, caste, race, or place of birth. It ensures equal employment opportunities in the government and against discrimination by the State in matters of employment based on caste and religion. This right also includes the abolition of titles as well as untouchability.

b] The Right to Freedom (Article 19-22) includes many rights, such as

- Freedom of speech
- Freedom of expression
- Freedom of assembly without arms
- Freedom of association
- Freedom to practice any profession and
- Freedom to reside in any part of the country

c] The Right against Exploitation (Article 23-24) implies the prohibition of traffic in human beings and other forms of forced labour. The Constitution prohibits the employment of children under 14 years in hazardous conditions.

d] The Right to Freedom of Religion (Article 25-28) ensures that each person has the right to freely practice their faith, establish and maintain religious and charitable institutions.

e] The Cultural and Educational Rights (Article 29-30) protects the rights of religious, cultural, and linguistic minorities by facilitating them to preserve their heritage and culture and,

f] Lastly, the Right to Constitutional Remedies (Article 32) guarantees remedies if the fundamental rights of citizens are violated. When these rights are violated, the aggrieved party can approach the High Court or the Supreme Court of India, which can issue writs for enforcing fundamental rights.

His Lordship bridged fundamental rights with fundamental duties for a democratic polity to succeed through citizens participating in the governance process by assuming responsibilities, discharging citizenship duties, and coming forward to give their best to the country. His Lordship's words of wisdom to the young budding law students highlighted that the legal journey is a life-long journey that requires strict adherence to the continuous learning process, re-learning, and adapting to different environments. Students were encouraged to actively participate in competitions and avail of internship opportunities to enhance performance in the practical world of law.

In the concluding lines, His Lordship ignited the minds of students with the following lines:

"A judge's life is essentially founded on upholding the law and ensuring justice for the citizens. My young friends, after completing your legal education, you all qualify to become Judges or legal practitioners. Different career options are spread out for you all in forging your future. Ambition, investment of time in your goals, and perseverance will lead to a successful future. This would be the mission for you all, as intended by the founding fathers of our Constitution. Lastly, I would like to leave you all with a line to ponder – "Let not your winged days be spent in vain. "After the speech, we had a brief meeting with the management and left for the District Court for the inspection by His Lordship.

I learnt the following during the meeting with judicial officers:

- There is a systematic process to reduce the number of cases in the District Judiciary. Each Judge in the room had the opportunity to speak and share their progress report.
- His Lordship carefully analyzed the report of each Judge to speed up the disposal of cases. A timeline was framed for follow-up meetings on the progress of work. Other Judges joined the meeting through video-conferencing for the discussion.

His Lordship suggested the idea of the judges availing internship opportunities for the speedy disposal of cases. I was called to be seated amidst the judicial members to whom I was introduced as an intern at the chambers.

After the meeting, His Lordship addressed the members of the Mysore Bar Association. His Lordship spoke on the unique history and tradition of the Mysore Bar Association and assured the members that the requests would be processed for the Chief Justice's approval. After the event, we headed for a quick lunch at the guest house with His Lordship being the Chairman of District Judiciary's Building Committee.

Attending the Event Organized by Mysore Bar Association in the Month of December - 2022

Picture of Chamundeshwari Temple

A divine visit to the Chamundi Hills, twelve kilometres from Mysore, is home to the Goddess Chamundeshwari, the patron deity of the Mysuru Royal Family. The Chamundeshwari Temple is considered a Shakti Peetha and one among the 18 Shakti Peethas. According to the legends, the Goddess defeated the demon king Mahishasura on this hill. The Chamundeshwari Temple received patronage from all rulers, such as Hoysalas, Vijayanagara Empire and Mysuru Wodeyars. A darshan at the temple with His Lordship as the Chief Justice enroute to Bengaluru brought a fulfilling internship experience.

Picture after the Darshan at Chamundeshwari Temple on 13th February - 2024

Recollection of Darshan at the Temples enroute to Bangalore after the First Visit with His Lordship to Mysore [2022]

Chapter 15

Dharwad Days

Chief Justice of High Court of Karnataka P.S. Dinesh Kumar and Respected Jayashree madam being felicitated in Dharwad by Bar Association, High Court of Karnataka, Dharwad.

His Lordship presided over the Kalaburagi Bench of the Karnataka High Court and visited Yadagir, Vijyapura, Belagavi, Chikkodi, Raibagh and Gokak in an official capacity for various inaugurations and laying of foundation stones en route to Dharwad. On the 18th of February 2024, I took a flight from Bangalore to Hubbli to attend the judicial sitting of His Lordship at the High Court of Karnataka, Dharwad Bench. I accompanied His Lordship for a walk in the scenic environment within the premises of the High Court. His Lordship recalled the days of being posted at the Dharwad Bench as a Judge of the Karnataka High Court. I could connect with His Lordship's description of nature's gift bestowed upon the city of Dharwad. The walk brought forth various aspects, such as the expansion and upgradation of judicial infrastructure and the path ahead for the development of the Indian Judiciary. The next day morning, His Lordship visited Sri Uttaradi Math, one of the main monasteries founded by Sri.Madhavacharya with Padmanabha Tirtha as its head to preserve and propagate Dvaita Vedanta in the region. This was followed by visiting Nuggikeri Hanuman Temple before returning to the court premises.

Visit to Shri Uttaradi Mutt

Felicitation and Offerings to His Lordship

Guard of Honour in Dharwad

Seated in the Official Chair of Chief Justice at Dharwad

The Judicial Sitting at the Dharwad Bench commenced with a Guard of Honour upon His Lordship's arrival at the venue. As I observed the ceremonial sitting alongside Law Clerks, I observed His Lordship continuing to quickly dispose of the cases within a short span of time, ending the session at 12.45 PM. This was followed by the virtual inauguration of the Judicial Officer's quarters at Kalaghatghi and attending the program organized by the Bar Association, High Court of Karnataka, Dharwad. His Lordship asked advocates to imbibe professional skills through continuous study and extend their cooperation to the judiciary to uphold the democratic sovereignty of the country by actively participating in the justice delivery system.

His Lordship recalled the association with Dharwad as an advocate and then as a Judge. His Lordship said that he had an opportunity to now serve as the Chief Justice of Karnataka. The Hon'ble Chief Justice and Respected Jayashree Madam were honoured by the Bar Association with a small statue of Karnataka's cultural icon Basavanna in the presence of various High Court Judges. I began the journey towards Bengaluru with a precious learning experience in Dharwad. It became the last official visit as an Intern at the Office of Chief Justice P.S Dinesh Kumar.

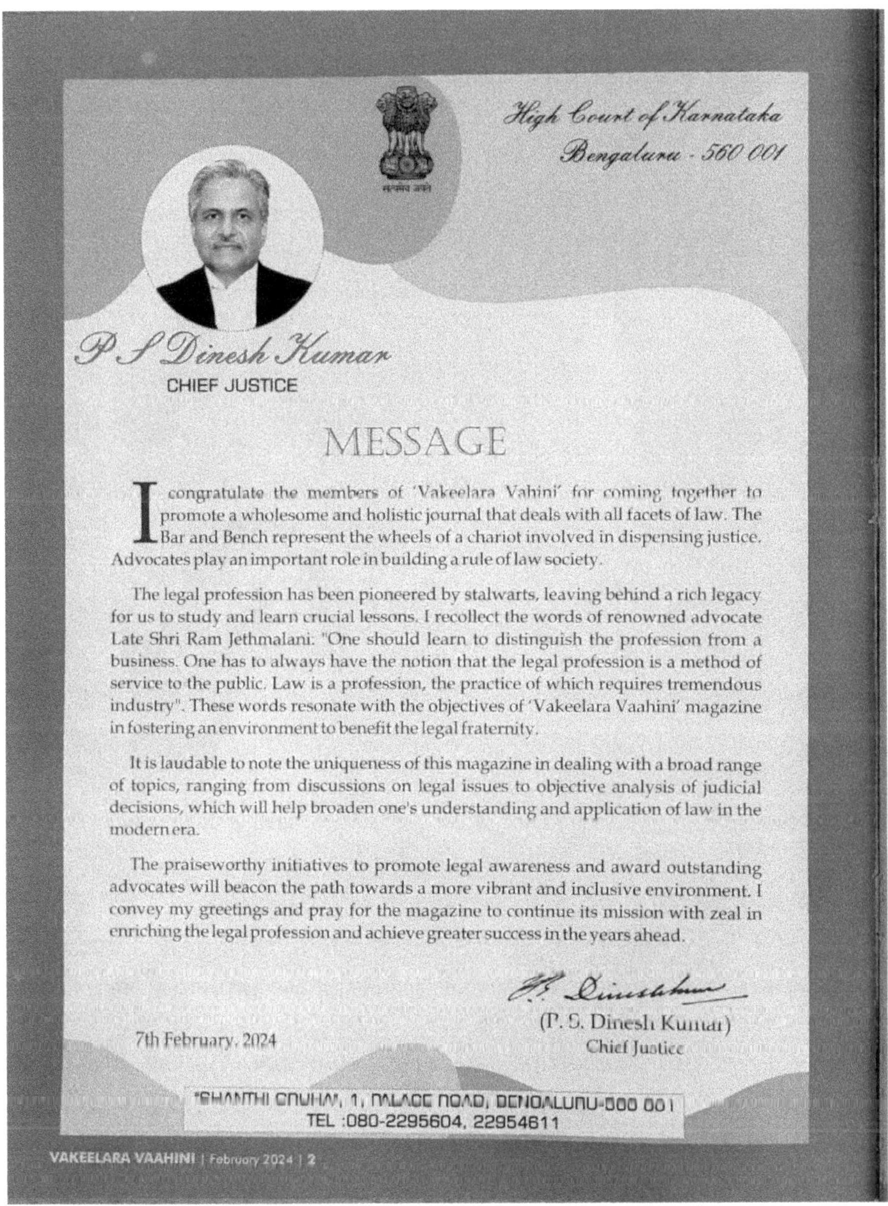

High Court of Karnataka
Bengaluru - 560 001

P S Dinesh Kumar
CHIEF JUSTICE

MESSAGE

I congratulate the members of 'Vakeelara Vahini' for coming together to promote a wholesome and holistic journal that deals with all facets of law. The Bar and Bench represent the wheels of a chariot involved in dispensing justice. Advocates play an important role in building a rule of law society.

The legal profession has been pioneered by stalwarts, leaving behind a rich legacy for us to study and learn crucial lessons. I recollect the words of renowned advocate Late Shri Ram Jethmalani. "One should learn to distinguish the profession from a business. One has to always have the notion that the legal profession is a method of service to the public. Law is a profession, the practice of which requires tremendous industry". These words resonate with the objectives of 'Vakeelara Vaahini' magazine in fostering an environment to benefit the legal fraternity.

It is laudable to note the uniqueness of this magazine in dealing with a broad range of topics, ranging from discussions on legal issues to objective analysis of judicial decisions, which will help broaden one's understanding and application of law in the modern era.

The praiseworthy initiatives to promote legal awareness and award outstanding advocates will beacon the path towards a more vibrant and inclusive environment. I convey my greetings and pray for the magazine to continue its mission with zeal in enriching the legal profession and achieve greater success in the years ahead.

(P. S. Dinesh Kumar)
Chief Justice

7th February, 2024

"SHANTHI GRUHA", 1, PALACE ROAD, BENGALURU-560 001
TEL :080-2295604, 22954611

VAKEELARA VAAHINI | February 2024 | 2

His Lordship's Message for the 'Vakeelara Vaahini' – A Bilingual Monthly Magazine

Chapter 16

Farewell Ceremony

Left to Right: Law Clerks Pooja and Preksha, Respected Jayashree Madam, His Lordship and Myself after the Farewell Address at the Karnataka High Court

The Twenty - Third of February marked a culmination of an illustrious career of Hon'ble Chief Justice P.S Dinesh Kumar. Indian Constitution mandates Judges of High Court to demit the office at the age of 62. A day filled with intense emotion and memories as I observed His Lordship continuing with the hearing and disposal of cases in the trademark routine. As the morning session ended, Senior Advocates seated in the courtroom rushed to the mike before the division bench stood to leave the courtroom. They unanimously mentioned that the Bar is grateful for the extraordinary service rendered by His Lordship in the judicial field. One of them quipped that the demitting of office had come too quickly, and they sincerely wished that it had been extended for a longer time. The Judges of the High Court gathered for the farewell ceremony at 2.00 P.M. The Bar and Bench bid adieu to the Chief Justice superannuating as the Head of Karnataka's Judiciary. The first court hall was packed with advocates standing on the aisles to glimpse the telecasted event. His Lordship addressed the gathering on the solemn occasion:

"Mr. Chairman and Hon'ble Justice K. Somashekar,

I am grateful for the kind words you have spoken of me. It is a day for me to recollect the distance travelled to bid adieu as the Chief Justice of this Court. My introduction to the legal profession began at a young age through my father, the late Pratinidhi Srinivasacharya, whose life as an Advocate and Judge symbolized intellectual aura and divine faith. I began to observe the role of Bar and Bench in the established process for administrating justice within our democratic framework. My aim to pursue legal education fructified with the wheel of time. Indian tradition revers teachers as equals to Gods by saying "Acharya Devo Bhava." All my Gurus have set a shining example by living an ethical and principled life.

In the year 1990, I began to work in the chambers of Hon'ble Justice Shivaraj. V. Patil, Former Judge, Supreme Court of India who imparted crucial lessons that the key to a successful legal career is built upon preparation and a strong understanding of law. Justice Patil believed in hard work and the blessings of people. I am most fortunate to have been guided over the decades by Hon'ble Justice M.N. Venkatachaliah, Former Chief Justice of India, whose judicial statesmanship has beaconed the progress of Indian judiciary. My association with the Former Attorney General for India, Mr. Soli Sorabjee, taught me the need to cultivate perseverance as an essential quality in the legal career. My horizon of legal knowledge expanded over the decades as an Advocate representing the Union of India and various prestigious institutions like UPSC, CBI etc.

The Bar and Bench are indispensable in the process of administration of justice. The life of a Judge is like a 'hermit in the forest'. In 2015, I took oath as a Judge of Karnataka High Court after practicing for two and half decades. I pledged my devotion to the sacred words "Yatodharmastato Jayah" inscribed in the logo of the Supreme Court, which reminds me of the revered duties of a judge to uphold 'dharma' at all times. My tenure as a Judge provided me an opportunity to serve the judicial system. I believed in writing easily readable judgments by using simple jargon. The judgment writing involves a solemn process to uphold the constitutional responsibilities. Judgments must be easily understandable by ordinary people. As a Judge and Chief Justice, it has been my earnest endeavour to maintain the highest traditions of this Court. Along with my team members, I have strived my best in improving the judicial infrastructure and systematically implementing the 'e-courts' project across the State.

The landscape of our justice delivery system is dynamically changing with the inclusion of technology, leading to numerous innovative steps in saving time and delivering justice to litigants. Karnataka High Court has an illustrious history with eminent legal luminaries contributing significantly to the development of various jurisprudences. I am confident that this great Institution will continue to grow and enrich itself constitutionally and academically. I am grateful to Hon'ble Mr. Justice H.L. Dattu, the members of the Collegium of this Court and Supreme Court of India for recommending my name for the judgeship; and Hon'ble Dr. Justice D.Y. Chandrachud, Chief Justice of India, Hon'ble Mr. Justice Sanjiv Khanna and Hon'ble Mr Justice B. R. Gavai, Judges of the Supreme Court of India for recommending my name for the post of Chief Justice. I am grateful to Hon'ble Mr. Justice

Bopanna, Hon'ble Mrs. Justice Nagarathna and Hon'ble Mr. Justice Aravind Kumar for their guidance and support.

I am grateful to all those who have been associated with me during my term of office in the High Court of Karnataka. I thank my Sister and Brother Judges for their fullest support and co-operation in my tenure as the Chief Justice. The Bar plays an important role in building a rule of law society. I pray for the Bar to continue its mission with zeal to enrich the legal profession and serve citizens needing legal services.

I appreciate the work done by the Registrar General and other Registrars who have helped me to carry out judicial and administrative duties efficiently. I extend my heartfelt thanks to each one of them. I place on record my appreciation for the dedicated services rendered by my personal staff who worked with me during my tenure as the Judge and the Chief Justice of this Court. I extend my gratitude to every employee of this Court at all levels. I record my appreciation to the Medical Officers of the High Court Dispensary for their timely medical advice and assistance. I place on record the excellent services rendered by Protocol Officers of the High Court in performing their duties with competence.

I am indebted to my pious mother and late father Pratinidhi Srinivasacharya for empowering me to pursue my dreams in life. I express my gratitude for the blessings of my brothers, sisters and all elderly members of my family. I thank my wife Smt. Jayshree Pratinidhi, son Mr Madhav Pratinidhi, daughter Ms Madhuri, and son-in-law Mr Amogh, for being the source of strength and support in my life. I thank my Gurus, relatives, and friends for extending their unconditional support to me throughout."

The Registrar General read out a direction by the Chief Justice on the sitting of the Courts at the Principal Bench, Benches at Dharwad and Kalaburagi as the Court arose with His Lordship leaving Court Hall -1 for the last time as Chief Justice. History would treasure the tenure of His Lordship, whose contribution has steered the progress of the Judicial Branch of Government.

Group Photograph with the Judges of Karnataka High Court

Farewell Guard of Honour to the Chief Justice

His Lordship had the same demeanour and a quaint smile while taking oath as the Chief Justice of Karnataka. I observed the same on the day of the farewell ceremony. It taught me the importance of leading an equanimous life with a calm and composed outlook for a successful legal career filled with legal prowess and perseverance embodied by His Lordship. I walked through Cubbon Park after the event en route to home with memories of my internship experience, that enabled a lifetime learning as a law student.

Speech at the Farewell Event in Vidhan Soudha

The term of office ended on the 24th of February, 2024. On the 24th of February, His Lordship was felicitated by the Advocates' Association, Bengaluru, at the Banquet Hall in Vidhan Soudha. At the event, His Lordship fondly recollected the brief stint with other Judges and the long period spent with Chief Justice Mukherjee. In the remarkable journey of 35 years, His Lordship was captivated by the world of law and subsequently joined the Office of Justice Shivraj V Patil. His Lordship deeply appreciated the Advocate General's words about the kindness and affection expressed by the Late Shri. Soli Sorabjee, whose visit to Bangalore on a Government Assignment as the Attorney General of India had left a profound impact on His Lordship. His Lordship served as the Assistant Solicitor General and, in this capacity, had the privilege of assisting him on behalf of the Government of India. The bond between them grew so strong that Mr. Soli Sorabjee would insist on contacting His Lordship, making some of the logistics easier, such as the stay and time of arrival, etc.

Mr. Soli Sorabjee would say to keep the gown and coat which has finally remained with His Lordship. Upon elevation to the Bench, Mr. Soli Sorabjee was closely following the news, and when the appointment came, Mr. Sorabjee permitted the oath upon one condition: someone must be deputed for the coat and gown with His Lordship's daughter taking the role as a qualified Advocate. The Chief Justice recollected such fine moments of life to cherish amidst innumerable incidents. His Lordship mentioned the plethora of learnings from Chief Justice of India [Retd] MN Venkatachaliah, who has been a mentor and guru for more than fifty years. Similarly, the lessons from Senior Lawyers such as Mr. BP Holla, who taught the importance of reading the bare act more than multiple times for a convincing opinion on questions of law.

Jamedar Shri.Sharabanna with His Lordship

His Lordship, with a mix of emotions, bade adieu to a profession that had been his life for about three and a half decades to conclude as the Chief Justice of Karnataka. His Lordship's belief in asking direct questions, such as the need for the person to come to the Court and the relief sought to determine the continuity of the case, was a testament to his unwavering dedication. After reserving the matters, His Lordship would ask for a one-page note learnt from the training experience with Mr. Soli Sorabjee, who always emphasized the importance of encapsulating briefs as a one-page note.

His Lordship's advice to the young lawyers was to have a proper conference with the client to prepare the brief by noting down the facts and relevant laws on the point. Advocates must consciously decide on arguments to present before the judge in a concise and precise manner before the Court. His Lordship underscored the absolute necessity for advocates to be ethical, as it is the key to earning the grace of the Court, irrespective of the decision rendered in the course of a case. Advocates are the first officers of the Court and then representatives of the parties. These qualities, if practiced diligently, would transform the Karnataka High Court into a model judicial system in the Country. His Lordship expressed his hope that if young lawyers start practicing such techniques, it will lead to a sea of change amidst the latest technology and computerization of the judicial system, with fine Judges shaping the foundations of our polity. His Lordship concluded the speech by wishing everybody a peaceful and prosperous life.

After the event, His Lordship travelled to the official chamber at the Karnataka High Court to complete the administrative work. An hour's work came to a quick end. His Lordship left the premises after 34 years of contribution to the noblest profession of advocacy by upholding the seven lamps of advocacy and fulfilling the sacred duties of a Judge and Chief Justice. As His Lordship was to rise from the seat of Chief Justice, I took a picture to treasure the moment.

Picture at the Office of Chief Justice with His Lordship on the eve of 24th February

As His Lordship left the chamber, I stayed back to pack my things and exit the premises. The Board of Chief Justice, with the name of His Lordship, changed to the name of the next Chief Justice Designate.

Office of Chief Justice

Roll of Chief Justices

The Website changed to include His Lordship's name under the list of Former Judges and Chief Justices of Karnataka.

A reality that took time for me to come in terms with the ever-moving and revolving wheel of life. The tenure of Hon'ble Chief Justice P.S. Dinesh Kumar came to an end with pomp and glory, which is now etched in the rich history of the Indian judiciary as the nation's finest Judge whose hard work and determination combined with divine faith led to reaching the height of success in the Judicial Branch of Government that has been steadfast in its mission to administer justice within the Indian polity.

Chapter 17

Shanti Gruha

Event at Shanti Gruha

Shanthi Gruha, the official residence of Karnataka's Chief Justice, is situated near the Vidhan Soudha with His Lordship utilizing the residence for completing administrative and judicial work until March

7th 2024. His Lordship asked the law clerks and myself to travel in the cavalcade for visiting Shanthi Gruha on February 14th 2024. A celebration by cutting the cake in the garden area and snacks provided a refreshing break within the residence.

On February 25th, 2024, His Lordship's 62nd birthday was celebrated by family members and chamber staff at the residence. His Lordship began the day by completing the dictation Judgements, after which the birthday celebration brought together a joyful occasion in expressing gratitude to the 34th Chief Justice of Karnataka. His Lordship recollected the numerous visits to the residence as a Judge while presiding in Court Hall-1 and spending time with Chief Justices to discuss various issues at Shanti Gruha.

Celebration of His Lordship's 62nd Birthday at the Residence of Chief Justice

Group Photo

The time spent at Shanthi Gruha was a blend of work and felicitation, by His Lordship and Respected Jayashree Madam. A special lunch was arranged for all the chamber staff and officers attached to the Office of His Lordship, as a token of appreciation for their service. Each of us, including the law clerks and myself, were individually honoured with the traditional Mysore Peta.

Felicitation by His Lordship to the Office Team

Meeting with Smt.Sudha Murty in an event enroute to Shanti Gruha

Felicitation of His Lordship by the Management of Shankar Electricals

Law Clerks and Myself take a picture His Lordship

His Lordship completed the judicial and administrative duties at Shanthi Gruha within a short time. The Secretary, law clerks, Jamedar Shri Sharabanna and others were dutifully present to assist His Lordship in the completion of work. My brief work at the residence of the Chief Justice added colours to my internship experience as the wheel of time moved us to an unfolding path in life.

Board of Chief Justice in the Official Residence

Lalbagh Walk

Walk at Lalbagh

Lalbagh is a sprawling botanical garden spread across 240 acres of land with two centuries of rich historical importance. Lalbagh houses India's largest collection of tropical and sub-tropical plants, including several centuries-old trees. An expansive lake and a beautiful glasshouse adorn the park, giving it a magical atmosphere. The Lalbagh walk with His Lordship provided me with a treasure house of knowledge as a range of topics ranging from law to science, health, and nature dominated the discussions as we breezed through the garden along with Mr Vinayak, a software specialist and Gunman Mr Reddy. I recall watching the show 'Walk the Talk' televised on NDTV. The walk began after the dictation of judgment, post-court hours as a Judge and Chief Justice of Karnataka High Court.

A Lake in the Backdrop

The walk at Lalbagh, ranging from sixty minutes to one hundred and twenty minutes, became a significant part of my routine after His Lordship›s superannuation. His Lordship›s pace was unmatched, covering more than 12,000 steps on a daily average. These walks, filled with insightful conversations became a daily post-college ritual. I look forward to sharing some of these conversations with His Lordship in the last week of March 2024 at Lalbagh.

His Lordship narrated the importance of out-of-the-box thinking by sharing ways to reduce and resolve the pendency of cases. Cheque bounce cases in India require to be distinguished where, in most cases, the party has drawn issued cheques in the initial stages but has subsequently resulted in a cheque bounce over time. If Special Courts are created for redressing such specific cases, that will ensure an immediate reduction and pendency of substantial cases covered under Section 138 of the Negotiable Instruments Act of 1878. His Lordship discussed the need to fasten the disposal of partition suits through the relevant sections of the Transfer of Property Act. The need for judgments written specifically to answer questions before the Court are necessary to avoid the scope for ambiguity leading to further litigations which need to be prioritized for improving judicial standards. His Lordship recalled handling a matter regarding the issuance of a bailable warrant against the Home Secretary with utmost perseverance in ensuring a solution to the case before the Court.

Conversation on the Role of Indian Judiciary in Our Democratic Polity

Completing the Lalbagh Walk

His Lordship's conversation was filled with unique insights, particularly when discussing high-profile judgments like the Antrix-Devas case. We even took a break to observe the sunset and discuss the systematic record in tracking the migration of birds. His Lordship shared countless anecdotes from his time as an advocate and Judge, each one offering a new perspective on the legal profession. The interactions with legal stalwarts and the narratives of their multi-faceted experiences significantly broadened my understanding of the role played by the Bar and Bench in the dispensation of justice. One memorable occasion was when His Lordship recounted a case representing the Former C.B.I Director Mr Raghavan, who now resides in Chennai. His Lordship graciously introduced me to Mr Raghavan, allowing me to engage in a meaningful conversation with the retired I.P.S. officer and Former C.B.I. Director.

Seated in the 'Red Garden'

After my introduction, the distinguished and respected Mr Raghavan showered his blessing and asked me to call upon him during my visit to Chennai, to which I expressed my gratitude. On several occasions, we travelled to meet Justice M.N. Venkatachaliah, who also felicitated His Lordship for his extraordinary achievements in the legal field. On one such occasion, His Lordship dialled the most eminent Senior Advocate, Shri. K. Parasaran, who spoke with the 25th Chief Justice of India, Shri. M.N. Venkatachalaiah, on the golden days of the Indian judiciary. After the call, His Lordship told me to seek the blessings of Shri. K. Parasaran upon receiving the Provisional Degree for registration in the Madras Bar Association.

His Lordship Wrapped a Shawl and Greeted Justice MN Venkatachaliah Before the Lalbagh Walk

Justice MN Venkatachaliah and Smt.Parvathi Venkatachalaiah Felicitate His Lordship

His Lordship's recollection of my interactions with eminent personalities like Justice M.N. Venkatachalaiah and Justice Shivraj V Patil was a testament to the personal growth and learning I've experienced. His Lordship encouraged me to stay connected with such distinguished individuals, as their blessings will be the most valuable asset in my legal career. His Lordship's magnanimous personality, following in the footsteps of Mother India's incredible leaders and personalities, has empowered me with the zeal and mission to live a purposeful life.

Left to Right: Gunman Nagareddy, His Lordship and Myself

The visit to M.T.R., a popular chain of restaurants near Lalbagh's Westgate, for refreshment after a long day of work is one of the fond memories as news of the notification as Chief Justice of Karnataka came to light at the same place on the 31st of January 2024. His Lordship had introduced me to Justice A.S. Oak, Judge of the Supreme Court of India, who was visiting Bangalore for an event. Previously, I had the opportunity to meet Justice A.S. Oak at the Karnataka High Court after His Lordship's swearing-in-ceremony as the Chief Justice of Karnataka. The walk to Lalbagh from His Lordship's residence covered about a thousand steps in the most incredible time at the 'Red Garden'.

Left to Right - Father Dr. Kathirvel, Mother Mrs. Arthy Lakshmi, Respected Madhuri Ma'am, His Lordship and Myself at the Lalbagh

A Picture with Justice A.S Oak, Judge, Supreme Court of India on an Official Visit to Bangalore

A chance meeting with Former Attorney General of India Shri.K. Parasaran.

Chapter 19

Securities Appellate Tribunal

His Lordship seated in the chair of the Presiding Officer after the Oath Ceremony in Mumbai

On 5th April, His Lordship was appointed as the Presiding Officer of the Security Appellate Tribunal. The Securities Appellate Tribunal (SAT) is a statutory body established under Section 15K of the Securities and Exchange Board of India (SEBI) Act 1992, to decide on appeals against orders passed by the SEBI. The SAT was created in 1997 to provide for a specialized forum for the expeditious resolution of appeals. Subsequently, the scope of SAT was broadened to cover appeals in respect of orders passed by the Pension Fund Regulatory and Development Authority (PFRDA).

The Securities Appellate Tribunal has significantly influenced the regulatory landscape of India's securities market, promoting clarity and consistency in the application of securities laws. A cornerstone of SATs mandate is to uphold the principles of natural justice. By providing a fair and transparent platform for the adjudication of disputes. It has enhanced investor protection and market integrity by ensuring that regulatory actions are subject to judicial review. His Lordship 's illustrious career paved the path to Bombay for a four-year period. The top position carried immense significance and authority. His Lordship's shift marked a conclusion to the destined journey in Bengaluru. I travelled with His Lordship to the ISKON temple in Bangalore on the occasion of Sri Hanumand Vahaana as part of the Silver Jubilee celebrations in Bangalore. On 26th April, I visited the Sri Govardhana Kshetra, a beautiful cave temple located amidst the busy streets of Basavanagudi, with His Lordship and family members.

Darshan at the Sri Govardhana Kshetra

Departure From Bangalore on 28th April - 2024

The visit to Lakshmi Narasimha Temple, Basavanaguddi and the innumerable temple visits combined with legal learnings gave me the empowerment to lead a purposeful life. On 27th April, my five-year legal education at the School of Law, Christ University, came to a successful end as I sought the blessings of His Lordship and Respected Jayashree Madam. His Lordship left to take charge as the Presiding Officer of the Securities Appellate Tribunal, whereas I headed back towards my hometown with an experience that needed to be penned down as a book which documents the journey of a student with the 34th Chief Justice of Karnataka Shri P.S Dinesh Kumar. I received His Lordship's permission to travel in the month of July for the opening of new building of Securities Appellate Tribunal in Bombay by the Hon'ble Chief Justice of India Dr.DY Chandrachud.

His Lordship receiving The Hon'ble Chief Justice of India on July 4th – 2024

Hon'ble Chief Justice of India Dr.D.Y.Chandrachud opening the new premise of Securities Appellate Tribunal on July 4th, 2024.

On the occasion of the opening of the Securities Appellate Tribunal, His Lordship delivered the following speech:

"My respectful Greetings to one and all present here. My Lord the Hon'ble Chief Justice of India, Dr. D Y Chandrachud, My Lord Justice Devendra Kumar Upadhyay, Chief Justice of Bombay High Court and your companion Judges all other dignitaries, my esteemed colleague members, learned Senior Counsels, Advocates, Ladies and Gentlemen: This is an historical moment as the Securities Appellate Tribunal is moving into a more spacious and well-appointed accommodation. This Tribunal was established in 1997 under the provisions of the SEBI Act, 1992, to hear and dispose of appeals against the orders passed by the Security Exchange Board of India.

The functions of the Tribunal also include hearing and disposal of appeals against orders passed by the Stock and Commodity Exchanges, the Pension Fund Regulatory and Development Authority (PFRDA) and the Insurance Regulatory Development Authority of India (IRDAI). This Tribunal plays an important role in ensuring fairness, transparency, and accountability in the Indian securities market with the decisions having significant implications for market participants, regulatory enforcement, and investor protection in India. Hitherto, the Tribunal was functioning at 14 th floor of Ernest Building in Nariman Point with one Court Hall. This building, renovated by the CPWD is more spacious with two court halls equipped with state of art technology for hybrid hearing. Inspiring leadership of Hon'ble the Chief Justice of India, Dr DY Chandrachud, has beaconed the progress of Indian Judiciary and witnessed a technological revolution and ushered in a change in the landscape of our justice delivery system. Despite his very busy schedule, when we requested him to kindly inaugurate the premises, he graciously accepted our request.

We welcome your Lordship. We owe you a deep debt of gratitude. On the occasion of the seventy-fifth year of the Supreme Court of India, Hon'ble the CJI emphasised on the need to cultivate a culture of professionalism within the courts to ensure effective and timely administration of justice. The Securities Appellate Tribunal is committed to steadfastly upholding the values fostered by Hon'ble the CJI. Since 2010, the Tribunal has disposed of 6768 appeals and as on date, there are 1024 appeals pending adjudication. In this new premise, equipped with advanced resources and technology, we shall earnestly endeavour to ensure speedy and fair adjudication while upholding high judicial standards.

We welcome and acknowledge with gratitude, the august presence of Hon'ble the Chief Justice of Bombay High Court, Shri. Devendra Kumar Upadhyay and his companion Judges, all dignitaries, Senior Counsel, Advocates and invitees."

Picture with Hon'ble Chief Justice of India
Dr.DY Chandrachud on July 4th - 2024

During the speech, the Hon'ble CJI emphasized the importance of the SAT and the Securities and Exchange Board of India (SEBI) in ensuring stability in the stock market and proposed the creation of more SAT benches to handle the growing workload. Hon'ble CJI stressed on the importance of effective dispute resolution mechanisms and robust legal protection for attracting investments and expressed confidence that the new office premises would empower SAT officials to work with renewed vigour and determination in reducing the pendency of cases. The event came to a fruitful conclusion with the departure of The Hon'ble Chief Justice of India to New Delhi.

Chapter 20

What Do the Law Clerks Say?

A Journey of Professional Growth: Reflecting on Our Experience as a Research Assistants under Chief Justice P.S. Dinesh Kumar, High Court of Karnataka:

Law Clerks Preksha and Pooja with His Lordship

Since September, 2022, we have had the privilege of serving as 'Research Assistants' under Chief Justice P.S. Dinesh Kumar, High Court of Karnataka. It is the day etched in our memory as we stepped into a realm where legal intricacies and profound experiences awaited. We were fortunate to be selected to serve under the esteemed guidance of His Lordship. The anticipation, a blend of nervousness and excitement, lingered in the air as we stepped into a new environment filled with opportunities and challenges. Yet, armed with determination, we embarked on this professional journey, fully aware that the complexities ahead would shape not only our legal acumen but also our character as an Advocate. This opportunity has not only deepened our understanding of the legal system but has also provided us with invaluable insights of the judicial system.

Our tenure under His Lordship encompassed a diverse array of cases including Taxation Law, Civil Law, Regular First Appeals, Service Law, Education matters, Habeas Corpus cases relating to custody of a child, Property Law, Contract Law, BDA matters, and Company Appeals offering invaluable opportunities for intellectual enrichment and skill enhancement. In the capacity of Research Assistants, our responsibilities extended far beyond conventional legal roles. From conducting exhaustive research on legal precedents to interpretation of law and assisting in the preparation of case materials, each task underscored the crucial role in preparation of a judgment. The understanding and interpreting legal precedents became our daily routine. His Lordship's inclusive approach, wherein he actively sought our insights and opinions, further facilitated our professional development.

We distinctly recall the moment when His Lordship entrusted us with our first assignment to research upon the relevant case laws on show cause notices under the tax law. The breakthrough in our journey was one particular assignment on Customs Law, which truly marked a turning point in our professional journey. After a week of thorough research and analysis, we prepared a substantial 20-page research work. This assignment set the tone for thorough approach required in our work. The appreciation by His Lordship not only made us happy but instilled a great amount of confidence and the curiosity to know and learn more. We were particularly touched when His Lordship placed on record his deep appreciation for our contributions to several judgments, acknowledging our research efforts. His Lordship has been very supportive and encouraging, throughout. The teachings were not confined to the walls of the courtroom. From drafting judgments like pros to understanding the intricacies of law, he made it all so clear. We have learned how to make complex legal concepts clear and comprehensible.

Beyond the courtroom, our engagement extended to observing the practical application of preventive detention through our involvement with the Goonda Committee. Witnessing firsthand the judicial process via video conferencing and engaging with law enforcement authorities provided invaluable insights into the complexities of legal practice. Additionally, we had the opportunity to attend various ceremonies and events, such as the swearing-in ceremonies of Justices at the Raj Bhavan, lectures delivered by eminent jurists, and other legal programs. We also visited the High Court of Karnataka, Dharwad Bench to witness the proceedings. One of the most unforgettable parts of our journey was a visit to Tirupati for darshan, organized by His Lordship. He ensured that the travel was comfortable and the journey was safe. This experience not only strengthened our bond but also highlighted the importance of balancing professional responsibilities with personal well-being.

Apart from the legal knowledge learnt, there are numerous other habits and virtues of His Lordship which has inspired us. To begin with, his dedication towards legal profession is unparalleled. We had rarely seen him taking any leave for a personal reason. He frequently discussed with us the significant responsibility that advocates and judges hold in society, emphasizing that every case should be read in detail, analysed, and interpreted with the utmost care to ensure justice is served. His commitment to these principles deeply influenced our approach to legal practice.

Our journey began in Court Hall No. 5 and witnessed His Lordship's elevation to the esteemed position of Chief Justice. Being part of this journey has been nothing short of a privilege. We will forever remain profoundly grateful for his unwavering support and invaluable guidance, which have not only shaped our professional lives but also enriched our personal growth. The simplicity, ethics, and commitment towards justice are values that we will carry with us throughout our careers. One thing that always be with us is his emphasis on integrity and doing things the right way. He has shown us that being a good and a humble person comes before anything else.

His Lordship had a profound respect for the value of time, ensuring that every moment in the court hall was used effectively. Before proceeding with any case, he would always ask the advocates if they were fully prepared. Only if they confirmed their readiness would he move forward, maintaining an efficient courtroom environment. He preferred concise and clear arguments over lengthy and complex ones. The questions he posed to the advocates helped to focus the discussion on the essential points of the case. He also encouraged advocates to simplify their presentations. He advised them to prepare concise, two-page synopsis of their arguments. This approach not only made the court proceedings more efficient but also ensured that the main issues of each case were communicated clearly and briefly.

Our journey was not without its challenges. Each work demanded a precise legal interpretation. The immersion in diverse legal research projects reflected a transformation of our skills and knowledge. The sharpening of legal analytical skills, improving of research methodologies, and the adaptation of nuanced legal concepts have equipped us with a robust foundation for future endeavours in the legal field.

Our journey as Research Assistants in the High Court of Karnataka has been transformative. The challenges met, the skills acquired, and the contributions made have collectively woven a narrative of professional growth. This experience has not only fortified my commitment to the pursuit of justice but has also set the stage for continued growth and excellence in the legal field.

Representative Image of His Lordship with the Karnataka High Court in the Background

Reflecting on our experiences, it is evident that our tenure under His Lordship's mentorship has been instrumental in shaping our professional identities. Each assignment and task contributed to our understanding of the legal system and our role within it. The rigorous research and analytical skills we developed have prepared us to tackle complex legal issues with confidence and precision. Moreover, the ethical principles and values imparted by His Lordship have become an integral part of our professional character. His emphasis on integrity, humility, and dedication to justice serves as a constant reminder of the responsibilities we bear as legal practitioners. The experiences and knowledge gained during our tenure will undoubtedly serve as a guiding force, influencing our approach to legal practice and our interactions with clients, colleagues, and the broader legal community.

In conclusion, working alongside His Lordship has been akin to having a guiding force and mentor of unparalleled stature. The steadfast encouragement, coupled with his profound insights into legal practice, has not only honed our professional skills but also instilled in us a deep-seated commitment to justice and integrity. As we venture forth into the legal landscape, we are committed to upholding his principles and values in our future careers, ensuring that the legacy of excellence and ethical conduct championed by His Lordship continues to thrive.

Chapter 21

Inspiring Speeches

Speech at the JSS Law College – Mysore

His Lordship's inspiring speeches cover a summary of addresses on different occasions, presenting a diverse reading experience systematically recorded throughout my internship period. Each speech delivered by His Lordship came with extensive research and preparation to ensure a fruitful session for the audience. His Lordship's speeches sparked and ignited the flame of thought, leaving a profound impact on the audience with a personal connection essential to the art of public speaking.

Speeches:

BM Sreenivasiah Memorial: As a distinguished alumnus of the B.M.S. College of Law, Hon'ble Justice P.S Dinesh Kumar addressed the management, teachers, and students on the inaugural programme of BM Sreenivasiah Memorial - 8th National Moot Court Competition. His Lordship spoke on the life of the visionary leader and renowned philanthropist B.M Sreenivasiah pioneered by the B.M.S. community by cherishing the noble ideals of sacrifice and service to society. It is notable that Sri B. M. Sreenivasaiah was conferred the title 'Dharma Prakasha Raja Karya Prasaktha' by the Maharaja of Mysore for his distinguished service in the education sector. His Lordship congratulated the organizing committee for striving to provide a platform for budding legal minds to showcase their advocacy skills and gain valuable experience in simulating courtroom proceedings. His Lordship's speech began with the recollection of sharing the dais with India's most eminent legal luminaries, Former Attorney General of India Shri Soli Sorabjee, and renowned advocate Ram Jethmalani for judging such moot competitions.

Over the course of the speech, His Lordship remarked to the students "I am sure that all of you can relate to what we refer to as 'case laws' that are vital to be learnt and applied for securing good marks in examinations. But there is something which each one of you need to ponder over that landmark cases were developed based on no precedence. It was a creation by the finest judges and advocates who presented their stand in Apex Court. Therefore, creativity and out-of-the-box thinking is a necessary quality as you pursue different careers in Law." His Lordship motivated each student to utilize such competitions and enroll for internships after closely observing interns in law firms, chambers of various advocates, tribunals, as well as with Judges in the Karnataka High Court! As students utilize such opportunities, the realization will set in that "learning law is a collection of experiences" - the more you participate and learn will multiply your knowledge and would better equip you to face boldly different situations that may arise from time to time. His Lordship asked the student community to develop the quality of self-belief to have a successful legal carrier amidst a technological revolution that has added to the spread of opportunities for 21st-century advocates to conclude an impactful speech for the legal world.

Speech on Alternative Dispute Resolution at the Karnataka Judicial Academy: His Lordship addressed a Group of Judges from Bangladesh about a significant topic which has gained increasing importance in our legal profession. His Lordship discussed the intricacies of Alternative Dispute Resolution and Plea Bargaining in the modern era. A general understanding about Alternative Dispute Resolution (ADR) refers to the different ways people can resolve disputes without a trial. Section 89 of the Code of Civil procedure was introduced with the purpose of amicable, peaceful and mutual settlement between parties without the court's intervention. The cases or disputes between parties shall attend trial only if there is a failure to reach resolutions outside the court.

The choices for outside the court settlement are between:

(a) Arbitration;

(b) Conciliation

(c) Judicial settlement including settlement through Lok Adalat; or

(d) Mediation.

The traditional mode of dispute resolution i.e. litigation is a lengthy process leading to unnecessary delays in dispensation of justice as well as over-burdening the Judiciary. In such a scenario, Alternative Dispute Resolution (ADR) mechanisms offer better and timely solution for resolution of a dispute. ADR mechanisms are less adversarial and are capable of providing an amicable outcome in comparison to conventional methods of resolving disputes.

His Lordship recalled that as the Chairman of Karnataka State Legal over 25 lakh cases were settled through compromise in the National Lok Adalat held on December 9 – 2023 in various levels of courts across the state. A total of Rs 1,569 crore had been given in the form of compensation. There was a total of 1,022 benches across the state, including three benches of the Karnataka High Court for conducting the Lok Adalat. A total of 25,14,343 cases including 2,24,080 pending cases and 22,90,263 pre-litigation cases were settled. I spoke on the expeditious resolution achieved through the Lok Adalat with matrimonial disputes seeing a high number of resolution while compensation totalling Rs 209 crore was awarded in Motor Vehicle Accident cases. 3,125 divisional lawsuit cases and 10,513 check bounce cases were resolved. Lok Adalats have been given statutory status under the Legal Services Authorities Act, 1987. Under the said Act, the award (decision) made by the Lok Adalats is deemed to be a decree of a civil court and is final and binding on all parties. There is no court fee payable when a matter is filed in a Lok Adalat.

His Lordship elaborated on Mediation as the best alternate dispute resolution method. It is a unique process in which a neutral third party assists two or more parties to reach an agreement manner and resolve their dispute. It is a confidential process facilitated by negotiation and mainly controlled by the parties. The procedural aspect is controlled by a Neutral Third- party and without any authority to impose a particular outcome. Mediation training is a structured programme. A trainee undergoes full-fledged training for 40 hours. Several important aspects and nuances of mediation are taught in the mediation training course. In order to be a successful mediator, he should ensure that all the parties are informed about the mediator's role and nature of the mediation process and ensure that all parties understand the terms of settlement.

Mediator should protect the voluntary participation of each party. If he perceives that a party is unable to give consent to participate in the process, he should not continue the mediation until the mediator is satisfied that such informed consent has been obtained from the party or the party's duly authorized representative. Mediator should not tender legal advice. He must also know about BATNA - Best Alternative to Negotiated Agreement and WATNA - Worst Alternative to Negotiated agreement. Having worked as a Mediator and a trainer for several years, large number His Lordship expressed that a large number of Mediators are doing an excellent job and the rate of success of Bangalore Mediation Centre at some point of time had reached close to 60%.

His Lordship expressed that if the cases are referred to a well-trained mediator, the rate of success will be much higher. Therefore, mediation training is, 'a must' for higher rate of success. The aim and object of every human being will be to live in harmony. Mediation provides for solution to the disputes with a 'win-win' situation. At the end of a successful mediation, parties not only resolve their disputes, but also restore their relations. In the era of internet, parties can resolve their disputes by online Mediation at their convenience. His Lordship concluded the speech by thanking the Director for the invitation and wished the Judges a bright future in their carrier.

Aryabhata Cultural Foundation:

The 48th Annual Aryabhata International Award Function recognized and awarded individuals for their outstanding contributions to society. His Lordship began the speech by recognizing that the award function has been named after Aryabhatta, an extraordinary teacher and scholar whose treatise Aryabhatiya has been was acknowledged as a masterpiece. The title of 'Father of Indian Mathematics' was given to Aryabhata, for his notable understanding and explanation of the planetary system. Cultural achievements expand the horizon of thinking and emotions in human lives. His Lordship noted the plethora of awards ranging from Law to Medicine, Social Service to Spirituality, Art and Dance as well as films comprising a number of achievers in their respective fields.

His Lordship recalled the words by Swami Vivekananda that "The true purpose of education is the manifestation of perfection which is already within us" with the ability possessed by the awardees to transform their talent by immeasurable hard work and perseverance affirming that a nation's best resources are its human resources. The awardees were motivated to create an impact on the lives of people by virtue of holding the key to national development. Nations such as Israel, Korea, Japan rapidly developed through excellent human resources despite lacking many natural resources. His Lordship noted the role of teachers behind individual achievements.

Indian tradition revers the teachers as equals to Gods by saying "Acharya Devo Bhava." Teachers set a shining example like Acharya Dronacharya to Arjuna, Ramakrishna Paramahamsa to Swami Vivekananda and like Siva Subramania Iyer to Dr. APJ Abdul Kalam, When the young Narendranath asked Sri Ramakrishna Paramahamsa whether he saw God or not, Sri Ramakrishna said that he saw God as clearly as he is seeing the person in front of him. This is where Narendranath became Swami Vivekananda believing in the words of his guru. India was a treasure house of knowledge for many centuries and since the time of civilization. India was the unquestionable leader in science, medicine, music, arts, and philosophy until series of invasions by outsiders which led to destruction of ancient universities like Nalanda, Takshashila, Vikramashila that were centres of excellence and had brought students from all over the world. Invasions destroyed the treasure of knowledge and educational system as it may be recalled that it took a couple of months for the invaders to burn the vast number of books at the Nalanda University Library.

His Lordship emphasized the responsibilities which each of the awardee needs to carry in the journey of life. It is the freedom enshrined in Constitution that has enabled each of awardees to work independently in respective fields. Indian Constitution enables each citizen to possess noble ideals in building our nation with determination to succeed in their intended goals. In every sphere of life, where there is a right corresponds with duties. The duty with each of the awardee is to pass on the talents to young pool of Indians. Training young aspiring citizens through acquired skills can be the best contribution for national development. It will have a significant impact in enhancement of young talent, thereby ensuring continuity of the art where young citizens can transform their intended goals into achievements in life.

His Lordship recalled a quote which says; "everyone has a purpose in life, a unique gift or special talent to give to others. When we blend this unique talent with service to others, we experience the ecstasy and exultation of our own spirit, which is the ultimate goal of all goals". This will further the mission to recognize arts, crafts, humanities, games, sports, languages, literature, culture, and values, in addition to science with forums such as Aryabhata Cultural Organization instilling a deep-pride of being an Indian not only in thought, but also in spirit, intellect, and deeds. His Lordship concluded the speech by congratulating and appreciating all those associated with the Aryabhata Cultural Foundation for their efforts in promoting and recognizing the cultural traditions of "Mother Bharat".

Independence Day 2023:

His Lordship Hon'ble Justice P.S Dinesh Kumar addressed the Judges of Karnataka High Court, Judicial officers and Members of the Bar Council on the nation's seventy-seventh Independence Day. Independence Day marks the sacrifice and valour of great leaders, statesmen and citizens who devoted their life in quest for freedom. His Lordship's iconic speech noted that seventy-seven years ago, we had unfurled the glorious tri-colour for the first time to fulfil the centuries-old dream of crores of

Indians to be independent from foreign rule. Indian history records the fact of people from all over the world having come and invaded us, captured our lands, conquered our minds. From Alexander onward to the Greeks, Turks, Mughals, Portuguese, French, Dutch and the British looted us and took over what was ours. His Lordship mentioned the battle cry of Rani of Jhansi Lakshmi Bai, Peshwa Nana Saheb, Tantia Tope in the year 1857, renewed with vigour and force later by Netaji Subhash Chandra Bose whose iconic speech to his troops was recalled:

"We must build up our national defence on such an unshakable foundation that never again in our history shall we lose our freedom. As soldiers, you will always have to cherish and live up to the three ideals of faithfulness, duty and sacrifice. Soldiers who always remain faithful to their nation, who are always prepared to sacrifice their lives, are invincible. If you, too, want to be invincible, engrave these three ideals in the innermost core of your hearts". His Lordship remembered our valiant soldiers and security forces, by thanking them for their bravery and commitment in the service of the nation. The speech marked the contributions of citizens who laid down their life in the fight for freedom and spent years in prison with the hope for liberation. His Lordship elaborated on the role played by Indian freedom fighters to gain freedom with well - founded and solid institutions to constitute, preserve and strengthen India into a nation governed by the rule of law. Freedom fighters from Karnataka contributed extensively to the freedom struggle. His Lordship noted with great pride that the first ever call for revolt against the mighty power of the British was given by a woman - Queen Chennamma of Kittur in Karnataka, which occupied a strategic place from both political and military points of view. She is one of the great freedom fighters of Karnataka who led a resistance against the British East India Company.

His Lordship highlighted the era of Maharajas and Durbars ending after Indian Independence, with an entire period spanning century now referred to in simplistic terms as "Pre – Independent India." Indian Constitution has been the guiding light for the progress of our nation. A document intended to shape the country's destiny aftermath of colonial rule resulting in plunder and depletion of our resources. The enactment of our Constitution became the primary step towards national development. The visionary document ensured that it includes the vastness and diversity of our nation with the formulation of formal structures to govern the citizens.

His Lordship asked members of the Judicial branch of Government, to spread the noble ideals cherished by the freedom fighters and framers of our Constitution. The technological revolution has ushered in a change in the landscape of our justice delivery system. His Lordship believed that a reformatory approach is the need of the day for speeding up our justice delivery system. His Lordship quoted the poem written by Rabindranath Tagore during pre-independence days. The underlying theme of the poem is absolute freedom;

Where the mind is without fear and the head is held high

Where knowledge is free

Where the world has not been broken up into fragments

By narrow domestic walls

Where words come out from the depth of truth

Where tireless striving stretches its arms towards perfection

Where the clear stream of reason has not lost its way

Into the dreary desert sand of dead habit

Where the mind is led forward by thee

Into ever-widening thought and action

Into that heaven of freedom, my Father, let my country awake.

His Lordship concluded the speech on the nation's 77th Independence Day by renewing the pledge to achieve the vision of a 'Developed India' by dedicating our life in the service of Mother Bharat.

Child Protection:

The Juvenile Justice Committee of the Karnataka High Court, in coordination with important stakeholders organized the event to foster a change in dealing with child protection. The conference had the active support of UNICEF. Hon'ble Justice P.S Dinesh Kumar noted that children in conflict with the law, prevention, restorative justice, diversion, and alternatives to detention is a broad topic that covers the causes of juvenile crime and remedies to ensure a crime-free society.

An act of crime by a juvenile is a product of distorted mind caused by multi-fold reasons involving economic distress, social plight, and toxic influences leading them to act against society. Circumstances inside and outside the home play a significant role in shaping one's life and overall personality. It has been analyzed that poverty and increased availability of information through technological mediums have led to juveniles being more inclined toward criminal activities. His Lordship shared the broad findings reported in various published papers and articles to understand the issue extensively. A detailed study reveals that petty crimes, in general, and heinous crimes, in particular, are being committed regularly in India by children. Crimes such as theft, burglary, snatching, robbery, dacoity, and murder are being committed by children below the age of 18 years. The data on the incidence of juvenile crimes is disturbing if statistics were the only criteria to measure juvenile delinquency in India. The figures from the National Crime Records Bureau (NCRB) indicated a steady rise in juvenile crime rates over the years.

His Lordship believed that every child has the inherent potential to grow up, achieve their full potential, and contribute positively towards the nation's growth. The Constitution of India grants children the highest priority for their protection and well-being. Indian Constitution in Part-III and Part-IV provides special provisions for the welfare and safety of children and women. A positive action expected from the State, to ensure the best interest of every child. Based on the constitutional mandate and the understanding developed in International Conventions and meetings, India developed its first legislation on Juvenile Justice in 1986. Moreover, there had been judicial interventions of the Supreme Court, especially through its judicial pronouncements in the "Sheela Barse Vs. Union of India" cases. These judicial interventions from the Supreme Court expedited putting in place updated legislation in the form of the Juvenile Justice (Care and Protection of Children) Act 2000. This legislation was intended to keep pace with international developments. For the first time, a distinction was made between a child as a juvenile delinquent and a child in need of care and protection. The fundamental principle, however, remained the same - to serve the children's best interests.

His Lordship drew attention to the need for collaboration between parents for primary prevention, which includes value systems, secure home, counselling, research, and analysis with the children. Effective trials and deterrent convictions from the courts can bring change.

Prisons need to be open institutions for correction and restorative justice. His Lordship concluded the speech by renewing the pledge to work with utmost devotion and vigour for the children's best interests.

Itinerary Court

Hon'ble Justice P.S Dinesh Kumar inaugurated the newly established Itinerary Court in the temple town of Udupi. Great saints, philosophers, and religious reformers of Karnataka made this place - Vaikuntha, the kingdom of God. The Supreme Lord Krishna came and stayed here in response to the desire of his pure devotee Madhvachaarya is one such narration in the blessed land of Udupi. His Lordship congratulated each member associated with the mission in expanding judicial infrastructure for benefit of litigants. The District Judiciary is foundational for the administration of justice to the litigants. It is the most accessible court, which serves as the primary interface between the justice system and citizens. It plays a vital role in upholding the rule of law and delivering justice. His Lordship recalled that from ancient times, lofty social ideals like justice, morality, and righteousness have received great importance in India. 'Punish the wicked, protect the good' was the fundamental duty of all ancient rulers. His Lordship noted that Indian Constitution represents a high watermark of consensus and compromise in our history - reflecting the best in our traditions, providing a considered response to the needs of the present, and being resilient enough to cope with future demands.

Justice Frank Furter of the US Supreme Court once remarked: "the Constitution is a dynamic process. Its applications to the actualities of Government are not a mechanical exercise but a high function of statecraft. Law is the vehicle by which society makes some of its most fundamental decisions, and courts are the institutions whose major task is to defend and preserve the order of things. Courts are an important part of society's institutions designed to set its norms within upholding the rule of law. As members of the Judicial branch of Government, each of us must take up the responsibility to spread the noble ideals cherished by the framers of our Constitution." His Lordship reiterated the remark that "District judiciary is foundational for the institution. Only if the foundation is strong the entire system can flourish. Judges and judicial officers play a very significant role in our Constitutional scheme. The common man always considered the Judiciary as the ultimate guardian of rights and liberties". The quoted words aptly summarized the constitutional obligations in the line of judicial duty.

Silver Jubilee of Newsletter Publication by Karnataka State Judicial Department Employees Association:

His Lordship Congratulated the President of the Karnataka State Judicial Department Employees Association and the entire fraternity of employees associated with the District Judiciary on celebrating the silver Jubilee of the newsletter's publication. His Lordship noted the role of Karnataka State Judicial Department Employees to steer forward the welfare of employees in district judiciary by improving the service conditions and motivating them to excel in their field of duty.

His Lordship noted that the reader has been introduced with the cover image of Lord Krishna playing the flute in a serene environment in the newsletter. The flute and peacock feather symbolizes knowledge and the eternal presence of the divine in our land's rich literary and cultural heritage. His Lordship applauded the efforts to include children of employees for allowing the expression of creative genius through the publication of newsletters. The speech began by highlighting the centuries of transformation saw where dynasties flourished and perished with the wheel of time. It is the treasures of knowledge penned by scholars resulting in epics, poems, and songs that preserve traces of our historical past. His Lordship recalled that the Karnataka is also the birthplace for Carnatic Music by recollecting the official visit to the ancient city of Mysore in the first week of December- 2022. It served as the capital city of the Kingdom of Mysore for nearly six centuries from 1399 until 1956. The rulers were patrons of art and culture. Mysore is noted for its heritage structures and palaces. In this era, Mysore Palace and the festivities during the Dasara festival receive lakhs of tourists from around the world. It lends its name to various art forms and cultures, such as Mysore Dasara, Mysore painting, and Mysore Peta (a traditional silk turban) has earned it the title of the Cultural Capital of Karnataka. His Lordship mentioned that focus of this newsletter to promote literary and cultural activities has immense historical importance for the present generation of Indians.

As part of the Karnataka State Judicial Department Employees Association's mission of motivating employees to excel in the field of duty, His Lordship shared a few cardinal principles in the course of employment for progressing up the ladder. Firstly, the ability to forge a positive outlook with hard work and determination will be the primary step in achieving excellence. A scientific example by mentioned by his Lordship captivated the audience. According to the Laws of Aerodynamics, the shape of the bumble bee is such that it should be impossible for it to fly. But the bee's determination to fly is strong. And hence, the bee keeps fluttering its wings, and this high-frequency vibration creates a vortex that ultimately enables it to fly. So, with determined efforts, employees can always succeed against established beliefs. That is the power of creativity. Secondly, persevere to enhance skills for excelling in the field of duty. "Skill training is a collection of experiences" - the more employees participate and learn will multiply the knowledge and better equip individuals to handle different situations that may arise from time to time. Thirdly, the focus must be on what is right before us each day. Excellence in judicial branch of government is a continuous process needing a creative approach toward executing individual work to the fullest of potential. His Lordship advised the employees to leverage modern technology for upskilling and using forums such as the publication of this newsletter for individual and collective contribution to the development of the Indian Judiciary.

Surgeons Day:

Hon'ble Justice P.S Dinesh Kumar addressed the President and members of the Surgical Society of Bangalore on the Surgeons Day program. The Surgical Society of Bangalore was established in 1973 to have an academic forum for surgeons of Bangalore in all specialties to share their experience of interesting cases and series of patients with a strength of 20-25 members. Presently with 1200 members exchanging surgical knowledge has led to strong knowledge sharing platform by virtue of the collective strength possessed by the institution.

His Lordship noted our rich knowledge in medical science by extensively tracing back the contributions from the Father of Surgery - Sushruta describing surgery under eight heads with basic principles of surgery such as planning, precision, and perfection find important places in Sushruta's writings on the subject compiled as Sushrutaa Samhita.

His Lordship mentioned the ancient surgical sciences known as Shalya Tantra. Shalya means broken arrow or a sharp part of a weapon, and Tantra means to manoeuvre. Shalya Tantra embraces all processes, aiming at removing factors responsible for producing pain or misery to the body or mind. His Lordship noted that Indian philosophy and ancient science, have always been very clear about health. Philosophy and scientific methods like Ayurveda and Yoga are born on this land. These curative methods are now getting international recognition. India is moving ahead with the confluence of ancient Indian practices and modern medical practices.

Doctors are beacons of hope and light to numerous citizens across India. Doctors have engaged in transformational societal missions to remove the pain and suffering of humanity. His Lordship talked about the Late Dr. Venkatasamy, for over three decades, is known for his silent contribution and for bringing light to thousands of people. All his life, he has worked to eliminate avoidable blindness. Dr. Venkataswamy implemented his principle that the Aravind hospital must provide services to reach the rich and poor, yet the eye care facility must be financially self-supporting.

His Lordship discussed the six important virtues to empower the care givers with a humane heart from a book titled "Medicine and Compassion" which medical practitioners must possess toward their patients. The first virtue is generosity; the second virtue is pure ethics; the third is tolerance; the fourth is perseverance, the fifth is cultivating pure concentration, and the sixth virtue is to be intelligent. The World Health Organization presents a comprehensive overview of the country's health system. It gives important information about India's robust health system, demonstrating varying levels across states. Our health care serves the needs of a country with vast heterogeneity in health and development indicators. His Lordship concluded the speech by reiterating the appeal of Dr. Venkatesh to all the surgical heads of various medical institutions for rekindling the interest in the young generation of surgeons to take up good scientific projects and thus improve the quality of scientific material being presented in the monthly scientific meetings & other prestigious platforms.

Our Chamber Team

Birthday Celebration at the Karnataka High Court

Hon'ble Chief Justice P.S Dinesh Kumar placed on record for the dedicated services rendered by Private Secretary Sudha, Assistant Secretary Yashodha, other staff members - Parimala, Anusha, Chaitra and Yashwanth, Court Officers - Roopa, Jamedar Sharabanna, Research Assistants Preksha R Lalwani and Pooja Umashankar, Peon Rangaswamy and Ravi, Gunman Nagareddy, Chauffeurs Dhananjaya, Nagaraj, Lingaraj and the staff members working at home office.

I am grateful to the Private Secretary, Mrs. Sudha, for the invaluable guidance and support during my internship. I recall the first meeting in September 2022, where the Respected Secretary asked me to be seated for meeting His Lordship and drafted the approval letter for submission at the Establishment Branch to begin my internship. I had the freedom to approach for any queries and help at the office throughout my internship period. The Chamber Staff of His Lordship were dedicated in performing their duties and provided a convenient work atmosphere combined with memorable conversations and events.

A Surprise Cake to Celebrate the Event

My twenty-second birthday celebration in the presence of His Lordship, Justice Shivashankare Gowda and Chamber Staff at the Karnataka High Court is a fond memory. The Navratri Celebration on October 19th 2023, and the visit to Tirupati on January 13th 2024, remain to be vivid in experience. We shifted to the Chief Justice's Chamber upon His Lordship's elevation and the felicitation at Shanti Gruha marked an eventful conclusion to the constitutional journey at the Karnataka High Court.

A Picture with His Lordship and Justice Shivashankare Gowda after the Birthday Celebration

Office Team:
Assistant Registrars [S.S]

KS Parimala

SP Sudha

Yashoda.N

Team Members

Chaitra

Roopa

Anusha

Pooja Umashankar

Preksha R Lalwani

Yashwanth

Jamedar Sharabanna

Peon Rangaswamy

Peon Ravi

Gunman Nagareddy

Chauffer Lingaraj

Constable Sharanappa

Constable Rudresh

Constable Lagamanna

Constable Sandeep

Home Staff

Vadiraj

Raghavendra

Rakshak

Shivakumar

Sources

1. https://www.livelaw.in/news-updates/public-sector-banks-permitting-large-exposure-without-adequate-securities-a-grave-concernkarnataka-high-court-169909
2. https://www.livelaw.in/news-updates/karnataka-high-court-dismisses-plea-challenging-antrixs-winding-up-proceedings-against-devas-with-rs-rs-5-lakh-cost-173405
3. https://www.livelaw.in/top-stories/karnataka-high-court-dismisses-amazon-flipkart-pleas-against-cci-probe-177994
4. https://www.livelaw.in/high-court/karnataka-high-court/karnataka-high-court-dismisses-petitions-against-police-sub-inspector-recruitment-reexamimation-242126
5. https://www.livelaw.in/high-court/karnataka-high-court/karnataka-high-court-gr-medical-college-mangalore-inspection-national-medical-council-article-226-constitution-246558#:~:text=Thus%20the%20Court%20allowed%20the,for%20the%20Union%20of%20India.
6. https://www.livelaw.in/high-court/karnataka-high-court/karnataka-high-court-directs-reconsideration-pay-scale-court-officers-251299
7. https://www.verdictum.in/court-updates/high courts/ibm philippines-not-liable-for-tds-under-income-tax-act-karanatak-hc-1462308
8. https://www.verdictum.in/court-updates/high courts/ibm philippines-not-liable-for-tds-under-income-tax-act-karanatak-hc-1462308

9.   https://www.verdictum.in/court-updates/high-courts/classic-case-speculative-legislation-huge-loss-judicial-time-specific-performance-judgment-karnataka-hc-1497812

10.   https://www.taxscan.in/levy-forest-development-fee-ultra-vires-constitution-karnataka-hc/12158/

11.   https://www.newindianexpress.com/states/karnataka/2024/Jan/05/bbc-discovery-netflix-to-face-contempt-for-violating-interim-order-2648000.html

12.   https://www.thehindu.com/news/cities/bangalore/karnataka-high-court-upholds-land-acquisition-for-nadaprabhu-kempe-gowda-layout-in.

13.   https://www.newindianexpress.com/states/karnataka/2021/Oct/02/karnataka-hc-upholds-amendment-to-co-op-act-2366534.html

14.   https://www.thehindu.com/news/national/karnataka/ls-polls-karnataka-high-court-notice-to-ec-on-plea-to-curb-use-of-tech-based-platforms-to-bribe-voters/article67804298.ece

15.   https://www.thehindu.com/news/national/karnataka/karnataka-high-court-asks-advocate-general-to-take-up-issue-of-parking-of-vehicles-on-footpaths/article67792937.ece

16.   https://www.deccanherald.com/india/karnataka/bengaluru/high-court-judges-surprise-check-at-bowring-hospital-reveals-shortage-of-outpatient-registration-counters-2826636

17.   https://starofmysore.com/karnataka-chief-justice-to-visit-city-this-evening/